Battle for the West

The top of the world. *The Methye Portage was the height of land between watersheds emptying north into the Arctic Ocean and east into Hudson Bay. This painting, by George Back, shows the northern end of the portage where it dropped precipitously to the Clearwater River. Public Archives of Canada (C-94110)*

Daniel Francis

Battle for the West

Fur Traders and the Birth of Western Canada

Hurtig Publishers
Edmonton

Hurtig Publishers
10560 105 Street
Edmonton, Alberta

Canadian Cataloguing in Publication Data

Francis, Daniel.
    Battle for the West

    Includes index.
    ISBN 0-88830-226-6 (bound). — ISBN
0-88830-227-4 (pbk.)

    1. Fur trade — Canada, Western — History.*
2. Canada, Western — History.*   I. Title.
FC3213.F72   971.2'01   C82-091202-6
F1060.8.F72

Printed and bound in Canada

Contents

Introduction

The fur trade spread into western Canada at the end of the seventeenth century. Initially Indians carried furs from their hunting grounds down to the trading posts on Hudson Bay, but in the eighteenth century Europeans began to penetrate the western fur country and establish settlements there. The high costs of transporting goods over long distances led to the concentration of trade in two major companies, the North West Company and the Hudson's Bay Company. These two competed for control of the West until in 1821 they merged. This competition spurred the trade across the continent all the way to the Pacific Ocean. The trade continued to be the dominant economic activity in the West until about 1870 when the fur territory was sold to Canada and new developments were set in motion. The story of these two centuries of trade is the subject of this book.

The fur trade period in the West is a well-documented era in Canadian history, but, for the general reader, many of the classic texts sink under the weight of their own detail. Furthermore, in the last decade there has been a great deal of academic work done on the history of the fur trade. This has taken the form less of new information than of new interpretations of what has commonly been known. For instance, women have suddenly been given a place in the trade, which formerly was presented as a kind of men's club. And the whole interpretation of the role of native people has undergone revision. It seems time, therefore, for a narrative history of the trade which conveys these new perceptions to a general readership.

The principal sources used for this study are the journals and letters left by the traders themselves, and it is best to state right away that these sources are wildly biased. For one thing, the picture they give of the Indian is often short-sighted and uncomprehending. But they are all we've got and if used carefully they tell us something of the native responses to the activities of the European traders. Something, but not everything. Readers should be cautioned that what follows is not an Indian history. It attempts to be realistic about native involvement in the trade, but it only hints at the rich Indian and mixed-blood cultures which flourished quite apart from the trade.

Similarly, in the great struggle for control of the fur empire, the sources are weighted in favour of the Hudson's Bay Company. The Company has bequeathed the historian a vast archive of records documenting the activities of its traders. Not so the North West Company, which left comparatively little. Much of the history of the trade, therefore, is told through the eyes of Hudson's Bay Company servants. In the past, this has meant that the Nor'westers have earned a rather bad reputation. I have aimed for fairness, and once again the reader is warned to keep in mind who is saying what about whom.

A short note on terminology. When I use the word *Northwest* I am referring, as the traders were, to the area west of the Manitoba-Ontario border, all the way to the Arctic. The word *West* is used interchangeably and refers to the same geographic area. I have chosen to refer to the offspring of Europeans and Indians as *mixed-bloods*. There is some academic debate about this matter. *Half-breeds* is considered pejorative. No one argues with calling the French speakers *Métis*, as they call themselves, but what to call the English speakers? Some prefer *country born;* others prefer *native born.* This is almost a matter of etiquette. I prefer *mixed-bloods* and hope it does not offend anyone.

Prologue

The fur trade is older than European settlement in Canada. It dates back to the earliest fishermen from Britain, France, and Spain who boldly crossed the North Atlantic in their small sailing craft to harvest cod off the eastern seaboard. When they came ashore to dry their catch in the warm sun, the fishermen encountered North American natives for the first time. Eventually an informal trade developed between the two groups, natives exchanging furs for the metal goods they had never seen before, and by 1534 Jacques Cartier described how the Indians came down to the shore holding pelts aloft on sticks and calling out for him to stop his ships and trade. "They bartered all they had to such an extent that all went back naked without anything on them," wrote Cartier, "and they made signs to us that they would return on the morrow with more furs." For a hundred years or more the traffic in furs remained a subsidiary activity, carried on by fishermen almost as an afterthought. Apparently the abundant supply of pelts in the American forests was not matched by a strong demand in Europe. But then, at the end of the sixteenth century, a change in European fashion suddenly created a rage for the broad-brimmed beaver hat and the Canadian fur trade took off.

A change in fashion might seem a fleeting basis for a trade which endured two centuries, but once the beaver had established its credentials it remained the pre-eminent hatting material no

matter how styles changed. The beaver hat was not a skin hat; it was a felt hat, made by removing fur from the skin, mashing it together and mixing it with adhesives and stiffeners. Beaver fur consists of two surfaces; an outer layer of long, coarse hair protected by an under layer of fine, smooth "wool." When both layers were intact the pelt was used to make coats but when the guard hairs were removed the underfur was perfect for making hats. The hairs were smooth enough to make a glossy finish while at the same time binding tightly together in a felt surface which stood up to repeated wetting and rough handling.

As furs became a valuable commodity in Europe, merchants began to visit the St. Lawrence River solely to trade for them. Marten, fox, otter, and mink were also bartered but beaver remained the lifeblood of the trade. Initially the Montagnais and Algonkin people were the principal suppliers, gathering pelts from more distant Indian groups to the north and west and bringing them to the tiny settlements on the St. Lawrence. But the fur trade soon made clear its inexorable tendency to expand geographically. As beaver in one area were exterminated, new fur areas had to be found. Indian middlemen guarded their knowledge of the interior well but traders saw the advantages of circumventing them and tapping the source directly. Competition increased the urgency of expansion, and the fur trade spread out of its cradle in the St. Lawrence Valley, moving up the veinlike rivers of the Shield toward Hudson Bay, then crossing the Great Lakes to reach the edge of a brand new country, the Northwest.

Battle for the West

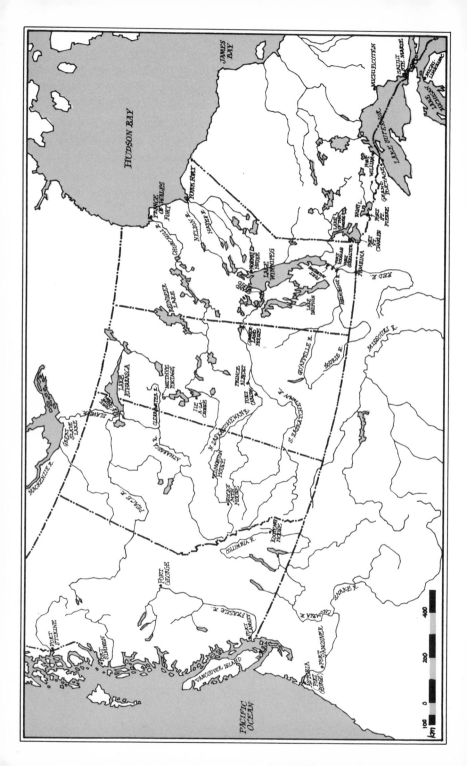

CHAPTER ONE

The French in the West

In the spring of 1726 Pierre Gaultier de Varennes, Sieur de La Vérendrye was forty-one years old. To his neighbours along the St. Lawrence River he must have seemed conventional enough, hard pressed like themselves to make ends meet, proud of his six children and the thirty-eight acres of farmland he had rescued from the thick forest. It had been fourteen years since Pierre and his child bride had come to live among them at the property on Ile aux Vaches, not far from Trois Rivières. They were a prominent couple to welcome into the neighbourhood; Marie-Anne was the daughter of one of the area's prosperous landowners, and Pierre's grandfather and father had been governors of the district. But there were no reserves of family wealth, and the young couple had to build a house and clear their land like any newlyweds just starting out. Pierre's first career had been soldiering. At age twelve he had entered the regular army as a cadet, and, after a decade of action in the border wars with the English colonies, he went to France where he hoped to improve his chances of promotion. At the Battle of Malplaquet against the English in 1709 he was desperately wounded by gunshot and sabre thrusts and left on the field for dead. After recovering from his wounds as a prisoner of war, the young soldier returned to New France, having learned that an unmonied colonial could not hope to keep up the social obligations of an officer in the continental army.

All this his neighbours would have known, but none of it contradicted the image of a gentleman farmer whose active years were behind him, settled into a life of rural domesticity among the seigneuries along the St. Lawrence. True, La Vérendrye dabbled in the fur trade at a small post up the St. Maurice River but after all, what colonist didn't if he had enough capital? No, there was no reason to suspect that spring that Pierre La Vérendrye of Ile aux Vaches was about to embark on a project that would carry him deeper into the western interior than any Frenchman had gone before; a project that would leave him ridden with debt, break his health, and blacken his reputation.

It began innocently enough.

In 1726 Jacques-René La Vérendrye, Pierre's eldest brother, took command of the *Postes du Nord* around Lake Superior. It was customary at this time for the government in New France to lease control of the far-flung fur posts to individual traders. In return for an annual payment, the lessee received a monopoly of trade in the district. He usually made an arrangement with merchants in the colony to put up the necessary capital for buying supplies and trade goods and getting them carried from Montreal to the interior. Under this system, control of the trade had fallen into the hands of a small number of merchants and administrators; obviously Jacques-René had good enough connections with this elite group to receive a lease. He asked his brother Pierre to come along as his second-in-command. Why Pierre agreed is not known. After all, forty-one is a little old to be subjecting oneself to punishing canoe voyages and bitter northern winters on an unstable Indian frontier. Perhaps Pierre saw a chance to make some good money at last; or perhaps the former soldier was finding domestic life a little dull. For whatever reason, Pierre agreed to go with his brother into the Northwest.

The *Postes du Nord* were a trio of trading posts, one on the shore of Lake Nipigon north of Lake Superior, one at Kaministiquia (Fort William), and one at Michipicoten. This was not as far west as the French had penetrated. In 1688 a temporary post had been built on Rainy Lake and soon after, nomadic *coureurs de bois* were trading on Lake Winnipeg. But Indian hostility and government restrictions frustrated French expansion and the *Postes du Nord* were the official limit of their western trade when the La Vérendrye brothers arrived there. Before too long Jacques-René, who was still an active soldier, went off Indian-fighting to the south and Pierre took command. As he traded with the Cree and Ojibway Indians who roamed the northern forests, and whiled away the long winter evenings in the company of vagrant *coureurs* who happened by, La Vérendrye heard fantastic accounts of the land which lay to the west beyond the Lake of the Woods. The Indians told him of a rolling prairie rich in fruit trees and wild game, inhabited in one spot by a tribe of dwarves. They described silver deposits and a small mountain of diamonds, "the stones of which sparkle night and day." But along with these fanciful stories, which the Indians liked to tell because La Vérendrye so obviously liked to hear them, the natives conveyed a pretty accurate picture of the country around Lake Winnipeg and the rivers which drained it. They spoke of "a great river which flows straight towards the setting sun," a river La Vérendrye knew to be the Winnipeg; they spoke of the Red River flowing north and south; and they spoke of another river rising in Lake Winnipeg and flowing westward deeper into the unkown country. As La Vérendrye listened to the Indians and carefully studied the maps they drew for him, a vision of the West took shape in his imagination. And he began to make a plan.

Europeans had always been unhappy with North America. They had not expected to find it in the first place, impudently lying across their path to the Orient, and when they discovered it was not just an oversized island but an entire continent stretching almost from pole to pole, they were infuriated. Initially the "problem" of America seemed simple enough to solve. There must be a way through it or around it. Expeditions were dispatched from England and from Spain and from Portugal and from France to find the inevitable waterway which would carry European ships beyond America to Cathay. But the inevitable proved impossible. The continent was seductive. It lured explorers up its broad rivers and into its inland bays, then it slammed the door. The rivers petered out; the bays led nowhere. Dead end after dead end was probed, then abandoned. Apparently there was no simple passage through this discouraging continent.

Perhaps, the newcomers reasoned, if they could not go around or through America, they could go across it. When they established their small colony on the shore of the St. Lawrence River the French had no idea what kind of country lay toward the interior. They knew that the ocean began again on the other side but they did not know how long it would take to get there or what routes they should follow to find out. Throughout the seventeenth century, explorers, traders, and missionaries from New France experimented with the waterways of the top half of the continent. Their travels carried them north to Hudson Bay, west through the chain of Great Lakes and south down the Mississippi River. By recording what they saw and collecting information from the Indians, they composed a picture of the "upper country" which was bizarre in its details but essentially correct in its broad outline. The French knew that beyond the Great Lakes the interior was broken by a height of land. From this height of land, they said, a great river flowed in a westerly direction until it emptied into the "Western Sea." Where the French were deluded was in placing the height of land within easy reach of the Lake of the Woods. As they learned to their dismay, the continent was much broader than they had expected. Each time they advanced one step into the interior, the elusive Western Sea receded two steps away from them. By the time of La Vérendrye the French had redrawn their picture of the western interior. Indeed, the Western Sea had become a gulf, like Hudson Bay or the Gulf of Mexico, intruding deep into the continent and opening onto the Pacific Ocean. The gulf could be reached by a westward-flowing river and that river had its origins in the land described by the Indians to La Vérendrye.

In 1730 the Commander of the *Postes du Nord* came down to Quebec to lay a proposal before the governor. Based on what his Indian informants had told him, La Vérendrye asked that he be allowed to embark on an expedition in search of the Western Sea. At no cost to the government he offered to lead a party of sixty *voyageurs* through Rainy Lake and Lake of the Woods, the so-called border lakes area, to the shores of Lake Winnipeg where he intended constructing a post. This post would be base camp for the expedition while it located the westward-flowing river. La Vérendrye had already engaged an Indian named Ochagach to guide him, and, since the project seemed like an inexpensive way of spreading French influence into the upper country, Governor Beauharnois gave his permission. On June 8, 1731, Pierre La Vérendrye with three of his sons, a young nephew, and a party of *voyageurs* departed Montreal for the West.

The Western Sea was only one of La Vérendrye's objectives, as the story of his explorations makes clear. He was, after all, a fur trader by profession and, not unnaturally, trade figured prominently in his plans. He knew that the Indians of the West, the Cree and the Assiniboine, traded the bulk of their furs to the English on Hudson Bay. If the French could penetrate the area, La Vérendrye told Beauharnois, they might intercept this valuable cargo and redirect it eastward to the St. Lawrence. But trade was more than a matter of imperial rivalry to La Vérendrye; it was also his support system. He was not a wealthy man and he had received only token support from the government for his western expedition. He needed revenue from the fur trade to cover his expenses and to pay off the Montreal merchants who had advanced him trade goods and supplies. In other words, exploration was going to be financed from the proceeds of the trade. This arrangement had unfortunate repercussions. A trading network took time and money to establish. Posts had to be built; transport routes had to be maintained; Indians had to be wooed by experienced traders; a regular flow of goods and supplies had to be assured. His masters expected La Vérendrye to press on into the interior like a conventional explorer, not pausing until he came to the Western Sea. When his expedition dragged on year after year with nothing to show but a lengthening string of trading posts, they naturally began to suspect his motives. La Vérendrye's most significant detractor was Count Maurepas, France's Minister of Marine, the official responsible for colonial affairs. Maurepas, undoubtedly believing that the Western Sea was just a short distance from the border lakes, could not understand why the explorer was taking so long to get there. He decided that La Vérendrye must be lining his pockets with fur trade profits to the neglect of his other duties and no amount of explaining by the explorer or his ally, Governor Beauharnois, would change the Count's mind. The result was that La Vérendrye could get no financial help from the government and was forced to rely even more on revenue from the trade. Late in his career La Vérendrye wrote plaintively to Maurepas in his own defence. "People do not know me: money has never been my object; I have sacrificed myself and my sons for the service of His Majesty and the good of the colony. . . ." Yet Maurepas held firmly to his belief that "the Sieur de la Vérendrye has abused his mission, and that for several years he absolutely abandoned his proper project, in order to turn his steps in the direction in which he thought he could trade to the greatest advantage."

That first summer La Vérendrye and his flotilla of canoes made their way by the Ottawa River route to the main trading depot at Michilimackinac, then pushed on across Lake Superior to Grand Portage at the mouth of the Pigeon River. At this point La Vérendrye ran into the first of many delays which would arouse the suspicions of his sponsors. His men, exhausted by the long haul from Montreal, frightened of unknown Indians, and mutinous for want of provisions, refused to go any further that season. The leader salvaged what he could by sending his nephew, the Sieur de La Jemerais, with a small party on ahead while he withdrew to the post at Kaministiquia. La Jemerais reached Rainy Lake where he and his men built a log post, Fort St. Pierre. The next summer the entire party came up and moved forward as far as Lake of the Woods where a second post, Fort St. Charles, was constructed. These posts were not the log lean-tos of the *coureurs de bois*. Fort St. Charles consisted of two small residences, one for the commander and one for a missionary, a church, and four buildings for the men, all surrounded by a double wall of stakes five metres high. Not only did he put up posts, La Vérendrye also had his men improve the numerous portages along the route. In best military fashion he was intent on securing his lines of supply. He can be pardoned for not realizing how self-serving all this activity appeared to the bureaucrats in Paris.

Circumstances conspired against him, of course, but even his admirers had to recognize that La Vérendrye was a curiously reluctant explorer. His object was discovery, yet for almost five years he did not stir beyond Lake of the Woods. He occupied himself first of all by trying to pacify the Indian groups living in the area. The border lakes region was inhabited by bands of Cree and Assiniboine who were allies in an almost perpetual war with the southward dwelling Sioux. In the past the French had not shied from stirring up hostilities for their own purposes but La Vérendrye came as a peacemaker. War was a costly inconvenience to the French. They could not keep a foot in both camps. Instead they had to choose sides, in this case ranging themselves with the Cree and Assiniboine and in the process losing the friendship, and the furs, of the Sioux. La Vérendrye much preferred a quiet frontier where the French could move in safety and the Indians attended to trapping instead of fighting. Initially he was successful but the Indians had no intention of allowing the French to dictate their affairs, and in the spring of 1734 La Vérendrye made a mistake which would exact a terrible price in personal tragedy. A group of Indian warriors appealed to the French commander to allow his eldest son, Jean-Baptiste, to come with them on the war trail. The exchange of children was a common way of expressing friendship and trust but La Vérendrye was naturally reticent. "Who could tell whether my son would ever return?" he agonized. The Indians were persistent, and the Frenchman feared being thought a coward, so in the end he allowed his son to go, along with a quantity of arms, on the understanding that the warriors would not attack the Sioux living nearby.

After settling this matter with the Indians La Vérendrye came down to Quebec to deal with his other pressing problem — how to pay off his debts and keep the expedition adequately supplied. There would be no help from the French court. Maurepas wrote snidely that once the explorer had reach the West "he will there, in all probability find new openings for the success of his enterprise." Governor Beauharnois luckily was more sympathetic and agreed that La Vérendrye should lease the posts he had established to some merchants in Montreal, an arrangement which would give him a settled income and free him to push ahead with exploration. Beauharnois remarked that "I warned him at the same time that, if I did not observe diligence on his part, I should be obliged to take some one else. . . ." Apparently even his friends were not above treating La Vérendrye like a child.

La Vérendrye returned to Fort St. Charles prepared to re-embark on his quest for the Western Sea. Unfortunately the canoes carrying his supplies did not keep up with him, and in the spring of 1736, when he should have been setting off for the West, he was instead dispatching his men back to Kaministiquia to collect the wayward goods. This convoy, led by Jean-Baptiste La Vérendrye, back from his Indian wars, paddled away from Fort St. Charles on June 5. None of the men were seen alive again. Twelve days later two canoes arrived at the Fort from Kaministiquia and La Vérendrye was alarmed to learn that his son's party had not been seen by them. Immediately a search was mounted, and on June 22, on an island in the Lake of the Woods just a day's paddle from Fort St. Charles, the men were found. Their headless bodies lay in a circle around a campfire. Presumably they were taken completely by surprise. One eyewitness who saw the scene of the murder reported that Jean-Baptiste "was lying on his face, his back all scored with knife cuts, a stake thrust into his side, headless, his body ornamented with leggings and armpieces of porcupine." La Vérendrye knew well enough who was responsible and his sorrow must have deepened with the knowledge that he was himself partly to blame. Despite all warnings, the war parties which he had armed and which he allowed his son to accompany two years before had attacked the Sioux, and now these Indians, full of hatred for the French, had exacted their gruesome revenge.

La Vérendrye was powerless to retaliate. The diplomacy of the frontier did not allow for settling personal scores. An all-out Indian war would mean the end of his expedition and possibly the end of French influence in the area. Instead he once again turned his thoughts to the Western Sea. A short time before he had sent his second son, Pierre, to build a post near the bottom of Lake Winnipeg. He had called it Fort Maurepas, doubtless hoping to flatter his chief critic, and it was to this spot that the elder La

Vérendrye travelled on foot early in 1737. After almost six years he had finally struggled free of the Shield country and reached the Northwest.

For years the local Indians had been telling the French about the Mandans, "the Sioux who live underground," a group of Indians who were said to speak French and have white skin and red hair. These people lived to the southwest on the banks of a great river, where, unlike their northern neighbours, they grew crops and raised animals. Perhaps the river of the Mandans led westward to the salt sea? La Vérendrye had come to Fort Maurepas to launch an expedition which would find out.

At this point in the venture the French explorer again displayed his inability to press forward decisively and with confidence. Pleading that his *voyageurs* refused out of fear to embark on the journey westward, La Vérendrye postponed it and instead spent a year making another visit to Quebec.

How astonished Beauharnois must have been to see him, especially since he brought only bad news. But La Vérendrye recounted his woes and apparently convinced the governor that Indian treachery and a lack of supplies were responsible for the snail's pace he was setting. The furs he was sending back to the colony must have helped his case, as must the slaves. These were Sioux taken by French allies in battle and sent down to Quebec where they were sold. There is no record of how many Indians were sent by La Vérendrye into bondage. In one recorded encounter enough prisoners to form a line over two kilometres long were taken by the French to be slaves. However, even Beauharnois's patience had its limits, and though he defended his commander in dispatches to France he told the explorer that he had better not turn up in the colony again without having something more useful to report.

La Vérendrye returned to Fort Maurepas, and after pausing to construct another couple of posts he launched his expedition west to the Mandans in the fall of 1738. Travelling on foot, the party of Frenchmen made their way slowly across the prairie to the southwest, gathering tents of Assiniboines as they went along. These Indians were making their annual visit to the Mandan to obtain corn, and by the time the caravan reached the Missouri country it numbered over six hundred men, women, and children. For all the anticipation surrounding this visit, it proved decidedly anti-climactic. The Mandan did not live in houses or speak French. They were not dwarves and they did not have red beards. They received La Vérendrye hospitably but he could not find out a great deal from them. Typically, his supply of presents was lost en route and his interpreter ran away when the Mandan, worried about the presence of so many Assiniboines, spread a rumour that Sioux warriors were in the vicinity. La Vérendrye stayed long enough to learn that the so-called river of the west in fact flowed south. Disappointed, he saw no point in prolonging his visit. The return trip to Fort Maurepas was the worst of the explorer's career. It was December. The cold was intense. His old war wounds crippled him with pain and several times the procession came to a halt while its leader lay in his tent recouping his strength for the next leg. "Never in my life," he confided to his journal, "did I endure so much misery, pain and fatigue as in that journey."

La Vérendrye did not abandon all hope for a southwesterly approach to the Western Sea. In 1742 two of his sons set off on an ambitious excursion beyond the Mandan across the Great American Plain hoping to find an Indian tribe which could lead them to the shores of the Sea. They returned without success, simply confirming the wisdom of La Vérendrye's other initiative; north-ward across the Manitoba lakes to the river the French would call *Rivière Blanche*, the Saskatchewan. At last La Vérendrye was on the right track, for the Saskatchewan truly was the river of the west which he had been seeking. In the years ahead it would be the principal highway of the western fur trade, carrying traders and explorers across the prairie to the foot of the Rocky Mountains. In the 1740s, however, the source of the Saskatchewan was un-known to the French. What attracted La Vérendrye was that the river obviously was used by the Indians as a main artery of trade. Furs were again taking precedence over discovery in his plans. He himself did not travel to the Saskatchewan, but he had his sons explore the lower reaches of the river, and, in 1741, they con-structed posts at Dauphin Lake and at the northwest corner of

Lake Winnipeg. Cautiously the commander of the *Postes du Nord* was laying a barrier of posts across the trading pathways of the West.

French traders like the La Vérendryes were the first white men to come into the West and erect trading posts there, but from the beginning they understood that they were in reality latecomers to the western trade. By the time the La Vérendryes extended New France's trading frontier to the edge of the plains, the Indians already had been carrying their furs to rival traders for over half a century. This was no secret to the French; it was in fact the reason they had come into the West. Their strategy was a simple one. If they could intercept the Indians on their way to trade, they could divert the furs of the upper country down towards the St. Lawrence and starve their rivals out of business. It was a strategy which relied on French experience living and trading with the Indians and their skills as canoemen and inland winterers, and there is no question that by the time of La Vérendrye it was meeting with a great deal of success. Rival traders complained that the "woods-runners" were seriously interfering with the flow of furs. In the words of one competitor, the Frenchman "not only beats the bush but runs away with the Hair also."

These rivals which the French were so seriously discomfiting were the English traders of the Hudson's Bay Company, settled in their posts on the distant shores of Hudson Bay. The Governor and Company of Adventurers of England trading into Hudson's Bay was created in 1670 by royal charter granted by King Charles II. According to the terms of the charter, a small group of London financiers and courtiers were given what amounted to their own empire in North America. In an area measuring 7,770,000 square kilometres, these men were given a monopoly of trade, ownership of the land, the right to make laws, establish local governments, and make treaties with the Indians. In return, the "true and absolute lordes" of the Company were expected to give the King and his successors two elk and two black beaver whenever a royal visit was paid to the territory. The price seems ridiculous now but it was established practise in the seventeenth century for European monarchs to carve up the world and hand the bits and pieces over to merchant traders who would then bear the costs of development. Usually these places were inaccessible countries with dreary climates and ungovernable natives, and royalty was just as happy to be relieved of the responsibility for colonizing them. After all, if the merchants struck it rich the King could always tax the profits. In gratitude to Prince Rupert, the King's cousin and one of the Hudson's Bay Company's original associates, the American territory was named Rupert's Land. Initially no one knew how large Rupert's Land was, not even the men who owned it. The charter was taken to encompass all the land drained by rivers flowing into Hudson Bay, but in 1670 no European had ever ventured up these rivers. The Company of Adventurers could not even draw a map of its own territory, and for the next one hundred years pretty well all its employees knew was what the Indians wanted to tell them.

From the very beginning the French disputed English claims to Rupert's Land so it is ironic that it was two Frenchmen who can be called the founding fathers of the Hudson's Bay Company. Remembered irreverently now as "Radishes and Gooseberries," Pierre Radisson and Medard Chouart, Sieur des Groseilliers, accomplished what few explorers can hope to accomplish — they fundamentally altered the way people looked at the world in which they lived. This was an act of imagination as much as an act of exploration but the French did not reward imagination when it conflicted with the King's command, and so the two *coureurs* ended up promoting their vision to the English.

In essence the idea was simple enough. During the winter of 1659-1660 Radisson and Groseilliers had wintered inland on a trading mission and in the spring they had met with the Cree Indians who inhabited the territory between Lake Superior and the "Northern Sea," Hudson Bay. From these people the two traders learned that furs were plentiful in the north country and they conceived the notion that this rich source of supply could best be tapped directly by sea. The sea approach not only placed traders squarely in the middle of the continent without a time-consuming overland voyage, it also avoided the Iroquois who were harrying French canoe routes all along the southern flank of the colony.

Radisson and Groseilliers had been trading without a license in the north and when they returned to New France full of enthusiastic ideas for expansion they were fined instead of praised. The trade in the colony at this time was tightly controlled. Officials were not keen on inland expansion and they knew that a sea route into Hudson Bay would be a nightmare to regulate. Undeterred, Radisson and Groseilliers took their plan to New England and from there they were invited to London in 1665 (the Plague Year) to meet King Charles. The result was that in 1668 two ships, the *Eaglet* and the *Nonsuch,* were outfitted to make the trip to Hudson Bay. The *Eaglet,* with Radisson aboard, was forced to turn back, but the *Nonsuch* sailed into Hudson Bay in August. Before cooler weather set in, a modest dwelling was put up near the mouth of the Rupert River at the bottom of James Bay. Christened Charles Fort, it was home to the crew of the *Nonsuch* that winter. The following spring about three hundred local Indians brought in furs to trade, and the *Nonsuch* returned to London with ample proof that Radisson and Groseilliers were right — Hudson Bay provided a direct route to the heart of the northern fur country.

Faced with this lucrative but unknown territory to exploit, the officials of the Hudson's Bay Company developed a trading strategy which took advantage of the direct sea links between Europe and the Bay while at the same time leaving undisturbed their own ignorance of the fur country and its people. On the shores of the Bay, at the mouths of the major rivers, the Company erected small "forts," draughty log houses thatched with grass or bark, caulked with moss, and surrounded by log stockades. Supplied by ship each summer with trade goods and provisions, the forts were the focus of the trade. In the spring the Indians from inland came down in canoes bringing their furs to barter. These furs were carried back to England by the supply ship and put up for auction. The rest of the year the posts were occupied by a handful of men who busied themselves hunting food, cutting firewood, and patching the buildings. These men, mostly tradesmen and labourers from the cities of England, did not venture towards the interior; they had neither the knowledge nor the inclination. They much preferred to cling to the safety of the seashore and let the Indians come to them. By the end of the Company's first decade a trio of trading posts had been erected around the bottom of James Bay.

The French on the St. Lawrence were kept informed by their native allies of English activity in the Northern Sea. Indians from the north had long supplied the colony with its richest, thickest furs and as the interlopers began to siphon off this trade the French realized that they would have to retaliate. First into the fray were, surprisingly enough, Radisson and Groseilliers. By this time seduced back into the French camp, these two enterprising troublemakers sailed from Quebec in the early summer of 1682 with two ships disguised as fishing vessels. Their destination was the Hayes River on the western side of Hudson Bay, which, along with its close neighbour the Nelson River, was a principal pathway to the western fur country. Radisson and Groseilliers arrived without mishap.

But the mouth of the Hayes River was destined to be a crowded spot that fall. As the Frenchmen prepared for winter they did not realize that on the other side of a low hill dividing the mouth of the Hayes from the mouth of the Nelson an expedition of traders from New England also was settling in. And shortly thereafter a third expedition arrived in the form of a Hudson's Bay Company ship intent on establishing a post. In all the confusion Radisson and Groseilliers took the initiative. They refused to let the sailing ship take refuge in a safe harbour and it was lost in the early ice floes. The few Company men who had managed to get to land were promptly arrested, as were the New Englanders. What authority Radisson had for his actions is not clear, but regardless, the French were now in possession of the area. Next season Radisson and Grosseilliers sailed back to Quebec, leaving a trading post and seven men. The story continues with comic flourishes. No sooner were the leaders away in their ship than a party of Hudson's Bay Company men from the posts in James Bay appeared and proceeded to put up a small establishment beside the French. This would eventually become York Factory, the head-quarters of the northwestern trade. While all this was going on in the Bay, the diplomats were mulling things over in Europe. The end result was that the French, eager not to antagonize the English, agreed to dismantle their fort and Radisson was sent the next summer to do just that. The mouths of the Hayes and Nelson rivers were left in the hands of the Hudson's Bay Company for the time being.

For the next thirty years English and French continued to feud over the control of Hudson Bay. Armed expedition after armed expedition was launched into the Bay and posts changed hands so regularly that officials in Europe and the colonies had trouble keeping up with events in this distant, ice-strewn sea. At one point France and England signed a treaty which confirmed the status quo in the Bay. The French would have the posts in James Bay and the English would have the Nelson River. But there was no such thing as a status quo. While negotiations were going on, the French captured the Nelson and since the English already had reoccupied James Bay the treaty actually accomplished the opposite of its intent. Finally the Treaty of Utrecht in 1713 settled matters for good by giving possession of Hudson Bay to England. The French were denied a sea approach to the northwestern fur country. If they wished to maintain a presence there they would have to find another door to the interior.

While the French and the English played out their rivalry in the Bay, the fur trade had been expanding relentlessly westward. From the few hundred native people who lived within easy reach of the early posts, word spread inland up the rivers of the Shield, across the parkland, and onto the western plains. More and more Indians began to make the trip to the Bay each season, bringing with them furs from as far away as the foothills of the Rockies and the Athabasca Lake country. Early each spring, while the ice slowly rotted on the waterways, they gathered at inland meeting places to manufacture the bark canoes which would carry them to the bayside posts during the summer. From northern Saskatchewan and Manitoba came the Chipewyan, a people so rich in furs that the traders would soon be calling their land the "Eldorado of the fur trade." From the forested Shield country which curled around Hudson Bay like the palm of a giant hand, and from the parkland which rimmed the plains, came the Cree people and their neighbouring allies the Assiniboine. These two native nations were the cornerstones on which the trade rested. Straddling the waterways leading to the Bay, they fell like a veil between the Hudson's Bay Company and the western fur country. Only obscurely could the Englishmen see past them into the interior and only gradually did the Company form an idea of the other people who lived there and how to reach them. The Cree and Assiniboine hunted furs themselves but more and more they took on the role of the middlemen in the trade, carrying goods from the trading posts deep into the interior to trade with Indians too preoccupied with their own affairs to make the long voyage to the Bay. When European and Canadian traders penetrated the West one of the reasons they did so was to outflank these Indian middlemen and put themselves in touch directly with the inland fur producers.

It was many years before competition from Canada pried the Hudson's Bay Company men loose from the safety and relative comfort of their bayside posts and lured them inland in any great number. But early on, the Company did try a single experiment in inland voyaging.

In 1690 an apprentice named Henry Kelsey was sent from York towards the interior with orders to contact distant Indians and convince them to come down to the Bay to trade. The Company had heard rumours of war and Kelsey was supposed to play the part of peacemaker as well, primarily so that the Indians "may have the more time to look after their trade and bring larger quantity of Furrs and other Trade with them to the factory." Not much is known about young Kelsey except that he must have had the boldness of youth. Travelling with Assiniboine guides, he was heading into country which no white man had ever visited, in conditions which would have taxed the skills of the most experienced *voyageurs*, to intercede among warring Indians with a reputation for ferocity. The results were hardly worth the effort. Moving southwest from the Bay, Kelsey reached the Saskatchewan River and the plains beyond. For two years he travelled among the various Indian groups preaching peace and the benefits of trade. No one is quite sure where he went but there is no question that with the help of his native guides, he accomplished a prodigious feat of exploration. Unhappily for his reputation, however, Kelsey was a man before his time. The Company was not keen on the outside world learning about its territory. His journal, partly written in atrocious verse, was suppressed and did not turn up until 1926. It came to be accepted that Kelsey was simply a headstrong boy who had run away from his post after a beating. The Company did not have any skilled travellers to follow up his initiative and anyway there was a glut of furs on the market. Kelsey himself spent thirty more years in the company's service but never again ventured inland. The whole thing might never have happened.

As it was, the first traders to follow in Henry Kelsey's footsteps were not Englishmen at all, but the French. In the half century after Kelsey's pioneering expedition French traders established a cordon of trading posts to the south and west of Hudson Bay, which, by the 1740s, the La Vérendryes were tightening ever so gradually around the trade routes leading down to the Bay. Inexorably the French were attracted to the north end of Lake Winnipeg where the Saskatchewan River empties after meandering across the prairie. This area, centred roughly on present-day Le Pas, Manitoba, was the hub of the western trade where all the major routes followed by the Indians converged. Here in 1741 the La Vérendryes established Fort Bourbon and prepared to follow up their probing of the Saskatchewan with more posts. However, the job the La Vérendryes began was destined to be completed by others. Worn out by his years in the wilderness, embittered at the accusations of profiteering which surrounded his name, the senior La Vérendrye asked to be relieved of his command of the western posts, returning to the colony with the modest observation, "what advantages shall result from my toils the future may tell." La Vérendrye's reputation improved with the poor showing of his successor, and, in December 1749, at age sixty-two, he was preparing to launch yet another expedition up the Saskatchewan when he suddenly died. Against the protests of his sons the western posts were given to someone else and the glory days of the La Vérendryes in the West were over.

Pierre La Vérendrye's accomplishments were great. His expeditions planted the first Euro-Canadian settlements in the West. He deciphered the complex waterways of Manitoba and located the "River of the West" which would be so important to generations of traders who came after him. He altered prevailing notions about the western territory and he laid to rest the chimera of an easily accessible "Western Sea." Yet for all of this, Pierre La Vérendrye seems now a forlorn figure, harried by his own irresolution and the grumblings of his patrons, unable through circumstances and character to take the bold initiative that would have silenced his critics. He was obviously a man of courage and endurance. He was also a man of great pride; he suffered greatly yet refused to whimper before his detractors when whimpering may have done him some good. However, he did not seem to inspire the respect and affection which leads naturally to loyalty and as a result his plans were often confounded by men who simply refused to follow where he led. Towards the end of his life he was given a captain's commission and decorated with the Cross of St. Louis so he was able to carry on a decently fashionable life in the colony; but he never received the recognition he deserved or the money he was thought to have made.

During the 1750s La Vérendrye's successors at the western posts followed his lead and concentrated on the Saskatchewan River but they made little progress toward the Western Sea. Primarily they occupied themselves with the trade and at this they were more successful. When the English trader Anthony Henday arrived on the Saskatchewan at mid-decade he reported that "it is surprising to observe what an influence the French have over the Natives." Most of the best furs went to the French and only the thinnest were brought to the Bay. The Indians appreciated being met in their own territory since it spared them the long trip to the Hudson's Bay Company posts each summer. They also, by some accounts, preferred the French traders to the English. The French were usually experienced *voyageurs* who had been apprenticed to the wilderness at a young age. Their skill with the bark canoe, their endurance, their ability to subsist off the country, all these things must have impressed the Indians. Often the French spoke more than one native language and showed more confidence and familiarity when dealing with the Indians. The English on the other hand did not stray far from their posts. Huddled behind their log stockades, forbidden by company regulation to have any personal relations with the Indians, they must have seemed a curiously suspicious and unfriendly group. Of course, the Indians had more practical reasons for preferring one set of traders to another. The French were notoriously liberal with their stocks of brandy and it quickly became "so bewitching a Liquor Amongst all the Indians" that trading sessions were the occasion for drinking bouts lasting several days. Hudson's Bay Company men were not abstainers but it was French brandy that the Indians liked and the English could not always get it. As a substitute, they concocted their own "English brandy" which was in fact cheap gin tinted with molasses, but they would not even drink it willingly themselves and certainly the Indians preferred the more "bewitching spirits" of the French. Brandy was given away as a present to the Indians, a kind of early loss leader, and it was also traded. It turned out to be ideally suited to the economics of the fur trade. The Indians were not really good consumers. Their needs were quite limited and they could not carry many material goods with them in their canoes and on their backs, even had they wanted to. The attraction of liquor was that it could be consumed on the spot. As competition between French and English increased, the price of Indian furs was bid up and since native wants remained pretty well constant, more and more of this increase was taken in alcohol. The effect of brandy on Indian society, however, should not be exaggerated. Apparently drinking was a festive activity confined to the trading season. It may even have had religious overtones. Except in rare cases, it did not become a part of the Indians' daily life in their own environment.

Another favourite trade item was tobacco, and here the

Hudson's Bay Company had the advantage. The Company purchased its tobacco fresh in Lisbon and traded it in lengths cut from rope-like rolls. Known as "Brazile tobacco," it proved a "bewitching weed" among the Indians, and Anthony Henday even went so far as to report that if the French had it they would completely control the trade. Henday was exaggerating. In fact the western trade was shared in ways convenient to the Indians. From the French they traded many lighter items which the *voyageurs* could easily carry inland by canoe. Then they took the rest of their furs to the Bay where they acquired the bulkier items provided more cheaply by the Company. It was a compromise which the traders complained about but could not change, and, as it turned out, there were plenty of furs to go around. During the 1740s, while its traders warned darkly of French activity inland, the Hudson's Bay Company was turning a comfortable net profit of thirty per cent per annum.

Anthony Henday's voyage to the interior in 1754-55 made all of this, and more, clear. Henday was the first European to be sent west by the Hudson's Bay Company since Henry Kelsey. His orders were to contact the Archithinue Indians (the Blackfoot) and draw them down to trade. Henday's account of his expedition was severely censored by his superiors. Before being forwarded to headquarters any mention of his "bed-fellow," the Indian woman who accompanied him as guide and mistress, was removed.

Indian women made Company officials nervous and post masters were ordered "to hinder as much as possible the detestable Sin of Whoring." Sexual mores and racism doubtless had much to do with this policy but so did the trade. Still uncertain about the intentions of the Indians, officials worried that women invited into the posts would act as spies and saboteurs, informing their menfolk of trade practises and opening the gates to assassins. Furthermore the Company did not want any of its men meeting privately with any Indian, male or female, because it might lead to private trading on the side. But Company men had no intention of accepting celibacy along with the other rigours of life in Rupert's Land and it was not unusual for post masters at least to keep an Indian woman "at bed and board."

In the case of Henday, his companion was invaluable to the success of his venture. Henday was a fisherman from the Isle of Wight, a resourceful man no doubt, as a conviction for smuggling may show, but hardly experienced in inland travel or Indian diplomacy. His bed-fellow is another of the many native people who guided white traders expertly through the western territory only to be excised from the record afterwards.

Even with his Indian mistress and other guides, Henday was embarked on a dangerous mission, at least so the conventional wisdom had it. The Blackfoot were rumoured to be an unfriendly and warlike people. Legardeur de Saint-Pierre, the French trader who followed La Vérendrye onto the Saskatchewan, reported that the land beyond Lake Winnipeg was populated by "an infinity of Nations more savage than can be imagined, from whom there is everything to fear" and Henday was bound for the heart of this country. As it turned out, the Blackfoot were friendly enough but they were maddeningly indifferent to the trade. It was October when Henday reached their territory in central Alberta. Arriving at a large village of about two hundred tents, pitched in two parallel rows, he advanced slowly down the broad avenue between them toward the leader's tipi. Displayed on poles in front of some of the tents he saw scalps hanging, long black hair moving in the breeze. The head man was seated on a pure white buffalo robe surrounded by twenty elders. As Henday seated himself, no one spoke. Solemnly, pipes were sent round the circle and each man smoked. These were followed by pieces of boiled buffalo meat served in baskets of woven grass. Then Henday's Cree guide, Attickasish, explained to the Blackfoot that the white man had come to invite them to the trading post at Hudson Bay where they could obtain guns and cloth and all kinds of other valuable items. These blandishments, however, were received without excitement, the Blackfoot leader answering simply that "it was far off and they could not paddle." After some more conversation Henday was dismissed. The next day he heard more of the same. "The Chief further said they never wanted food, as they followed the Buffalo and killed them with the Bows and Arrows; and he was informed the Natives that frequented the Settlements, were of-

33

tentimes starved on their journey." This was quite true, as was the chief's logic. There was no reason for the Blackfoot, a people who did not use the canoe, to journey to the distant Bay. Whatever furs they had were traded to Indian middlemen. As for the Company's trade goods, they really did not need them.

Henday passed the winter on the plains and in the spring he and his party paddled back down the Saskatchewan and onto York Fort. At the Bay he reported that the Blackfoot "are very kind people" but were content to hunt the buffalo, which were so numerous that Henday passed through them like a boat through water, and they would not be persuaded to visit the posts. Having stopped at the French settlements on the Saskatchewan, he also reported that they were getting the best of the trade from the Cree and Assiniboine.

There was little the Hudson's Bay Company could do about the Blackfoot but the French were a different matter. Other inland voyagers were dispatched to live among the Indians and coax them into the Company's camp. This policy began to bear fruit and fur returns were growing when the decisive blow fell. In 1759 James Wolfe and his soldiers scampered up the cliffside onto the Plains of Abraham and captured Quebec. The next year Montreal was occupied. Cut off from their sources of supply, French traders could only withdraw, abandoning their mouldering cabins to the elements and leaving the western fur trade in the hands of the Hudson's Bay Company.

CHAPTER TWO

Pedlars from Quebec

The conquest of New France by British arms did not greatly disrupt the fur trade in the West. Traders from Canada abandoned their posts but Englishmen from Hudson Bay continued to visit the interior regularly, and, though the advantages of competition were lost to the Indians, the hiatus turned out to be short one. After the conquest the new British government briefly closed the western territory to trade and an Indian uprising led by the Ottawa chief, Pontiac, further delayed a return to normalcy, but once peace returned to the frontier, traders reappeared, and, despite attempts to regulate their activities, they were soon wandering freely across the West in search of furs. By late in the 1760s canoes from the St. Lawrence once again were seen on Lake Winnipeg and the Saskatchewan River.

It was not difficult for the newcomers to re-establish trade in the West. They followed the well-worn routes pioneered by the La Vérendryes, and in the seigneuries along the St. Lawrence they could draw for their manpower on a labour pool of canoemen who had learned the skills of the trade over several generations. Some of the newcomers were Frenchmen left over from the early days of the trade; others were Scots and Englishmen newly arrived in the colony with a stock of capital and a thirst for adventure; and others were New Englanders, experienced in the Mississippi trade, who had moved north in search of better quality furs and a more settled political climate. There was Franceways, the wily old Frenchman who had been on the Saskatchewan with the La Vérendryes; there was James Finlay, one of the first of the newcomers to winter in the West; there were the Frobisher brothers who probed the headwaters of the Churchill River; and Peter Pond who first crossed the height of land into the Athabasca country, and Peter Pangman and Charles Patterson and Booty Graves. The list continues, but, in fact, they were not all that numerous. In any one season in the sixties and seventies there may have been a dozen independent traders in the West. Yet, as far as their competitors were concerned, they seemed to be everywhere, befriending the Indians, "engrossing" the trade, and cutting off the flow of furs at its very source. And so, because of their independence and mobility and enterprise, they earned for themselves the nickname "Pedlars from Quebec."

In order to reach the trading grounds of the West the pedlars had to travel over three thousand kilometres from the St. Lawrence to the outlet of the Saskatchewan River in Lake Winnipeg. It was impossible to make such a trip each summer and still have time to barter for furs and return again to Quebec. The logistics of the trade forced the Canadians to organize a two-stage transportation network to overcome distance and a system of business partnerships to share the risks. Basically, a trading voyage involved two, possibly three interests. In Montreal a merchant took care of importing trade goods and forwarding them inland. He advanced these goods on credit to the pedlar, or winterer, who carried on the actual trading in the interior. Each spring furs were carried out to Montreal where the merchant shipped them to Europe for sale. In the early years Michilimackinac had been the *entrepôt* of the trade — the winterers gathered there each summer to pick up their goods and deliver their furs — but as traders plunged deeper into the Northwest the depot was moved to Grand Portage at the head of Lake Superior so they would have plenty of time to get back to their inland posts before freeze-up. Often this necessitated a third partner in the enterprise to trans-ship cargo back and forth.

A Canadian trading party consisted of several heavily laden

canoes led by a pedlar and manned by French-Canadian *voyageurs*. Each canoe carried about four paddlers and at times there were three hundred or more of these interlopers wintering in the West. The country through which they travelled was not always bountiful with game, and the men often arrived at their posts much reduced by hunger. Fish was the staple item in their diet, but it was time consuming to be continually stopping to set nets so the brigades tended to rely on provisions traded from the Indians. A *voyageur's* contract did not include three square meals a day, and after they arrived at their wintering places the men divided into small groups which dispersed through the country to fend for themselves. A typical post was described as "a long square; built log on log: half of it is appropriated to the use of the kitchen: the other half used as a trading room and Bed room; with a loft above, the whole length of the building where he lays his furs: also three small log houses; the Men's apartments: the whole enclosed with ten feet Stockades, forming a square about twenty yards." Here pedlars passed the monotonous winter months trading furs and living on a diet of partridges, rabbit, moose flesh, and whitefish.

The pedlars quickly came to focus their activities on the Saskatchewan River, the great "river of the west" located by the French. It was the main artery of the trade flowing down to Hudson Bay and the newcomers quickly monopolized the furs for themselves. Hudson's Bay Company men at their bayside posts regularly reported that the pedlars were "swarming" inland and cutting off the trade. "They have Canoes and men at every Place where Indians resort," complained one competitor, "so that an Indian cannot come from any part of the country but they see of them." Like the French before them, the Canadians carried the trade directly to the Indian tents. They were liberal with their liquor and flexible with their prices and apparently not timid about knocking heads to get their way. Yearly they advanced further up the North Saskatchewan until by 1778 they were wintering on the river halfway across the prairie towards the Rockies. At the same time, slightly to the north, they also were intercepting the trade of the Churchill River, down which the

Chipewyan brought their furs, and laying the basis for their greatest accomplishment, the leap across the height of land into the Athabasca Lake country.

All this activity left the Hudson's Bay Company a little breathless. Ever since the French had first begun to intercept its trade "back of the Bay," the Company had sent regular expeditions to the interior and this policy was continued with the arrival of the pedlars, but it met only limited success. The inland travellers were dispatched as emissaries, not traders. Their job was to lure the Indians down to the posts with their furs. But such a policy was of no use in the face of dozens of active "Canadian pilferers" willing to save the Indians the time and trouble of a long voyage to the Bay. At York Fort, where fur returns had dropped by forty-two per cent in 1768, post master Ferdinand Jacobs decided it was time the Company woke from its "sleep by the frozen sea" and established a small outpost in the Saskatchewan country. Initially Jacobs's London employers saw only the problems inherent in this suggestion and none of the possibilities. However, early in the next decade minds were changed, and the Company decided to commit its resources to a head-to-head competition for the trade of the back country. It was a fateful decision. There are those who argue that if it had not been taken the Company would have lost its grip on the western trade and the entire history of the area would have been different. Regardless, by deciding on inland settlement the Company initiated an era of competition which continued for fifty years and which was the motive force behind the spread of the trade up every coulee and canyon in the West.

The man chosen to oversee the establishment of the new post was Samuel Hearne. Hearne had proven his capacity for inland journeying by travelling across the northern barren-lands to the Coppermine River just a couple of years before, and in June 1774 he left York Fort in command of several canoes bound for the Saskatchewan. He reached his destination without mishap, and, even though the Indians told him that "the Pedlars by this time had to much influence, and that I ware to late in comeing," he took the time to scout out several possible sites for a post before fixing on the shores of Pine Island Lake just off the main channel of the river. "I determin'd to build the house, at least for the insewing winter, at a Part Call'd Pine Island Lake — it is the general opinion of those Indians that that Part will be more comodious both for Drawing the Indians to trade as well as for Provisions. . . ." That winter, huddled in their hastily erected log tents, Hearne's men learned the hard way about wintering out in the fur country. They were a batch of green hands to begin with, their leader admitting that "none of them ever having ben farther from the forts than a Wooding or hunting Tent," and the winter was a particularly hard one. By February the daily ration was reduced to a few ounces of dried meat and Hearne wrote: "This scanty way of living. . . is so alarming to my men in general, that it is with the greatest difficulty I can Perswade them from thinking that Entire famine must Ensew." However, local Indians came to the rescue with food, and in the spring Hearne returned to the Bay with a decent cargo of furs, convinced that the Company had no choice but to prosecute the trade "after the Canadian manner."

Aside from a late start, the Hudson's Bay Company appeared to have all the advantages in its competition with the Canadian pedlars. Hearne's settlement, called Cumberland House, was only 720 kilometres from its supply base at York Fort, and a brigade of canoes could make the trip easily in days while the pedlars were several months from Montreal. Furthermore, the independent traders from Quebec could not hope to match the resources of the British chartered company. Nevertheless, the Company laboured under important difficulties. First of all there was in the beginning a shortage of skilled manpower, caused partly by the lack of recruits from war-torn Europe but also by the general inferiority of Company servants. Company post masters decried the morals of the pedlars and "the set of abandoned villians" they hired, but they had to admit that Canadian *voyageurs* were superior canoemen and inland travellers. "The Canadians are chosen Men inured to hardships and fatigue, under which most of Your Present Servants would sink," reported Andrew Graham to the London committee. By contrast most of the Company men were recruited from the Orkney Islands and had no knowledge of canoeing, hunting, trapping, or dealing with Indians. In time they would learn these skills, but for the moment their inexperience put the Company at a disadvantage. As well as a lack of dependable labourers, the Company lacked the essential item for ferrying goods between the Bay and the Saskatchewan — bark canoes. York Fort was situated too far north for the birch to grow, and even if the raw material had been plentiful there were no skilled canoemakers at the post.

For all these services the Company came to rely on the Indian people. Indian guides knew the speediest routes inland. Indian craftsmen fashioned the bark canoes and kept them in repair. Indian hunters paddled the canoes and hauled goods across the troublesome portages. Yet for all they relied on the native voyagers, Company servants held them in low regard. Too independent to act the docile employees, the Indians often pilfered provisions as the brigades made their way inland, caused delays while they feasted and partied, and even abandoned the Europeans if more pressing business called them away. The voyages inland seem to have been a bit of a lark to the Indians while of course the Company men were deadly serious.

In his second season in command, Samuel Hearne described a trip upriver to Cumberland House during which he discovered that his Indian helpers had been systematically draining the brandy kegs for their own use and refilling them with water. Such sabotage must have been maddening, but the native people simply did not place a very high priority on the welfare of the Hudson's Bay Company. They had their own seasonal cycle of activities and their own families to support. Inland voyaging gave them a bit of added "income" in the form of tobacco, liquor, and some food items, but it was not important enough to them to disrupt their traditional way of life.

The establishment of Cumberland House was the beginning, not the end, of inland expansion for the Hudson's Bay Company. No sooner had the post been built than traders there realized they would have to go further. The problem was, as always, the pedlars. They set up shop in a large circle of huts around the new post and intercepted the trading Indians, until the master at Cumberland House cried out in frustration that "even those that may come

40

through the Pedlars most of them will be fleeced of a great part of their Furs."

"Out settlements" appeared to be the only answer, small tents of a few men who would go beyond the Canadians and be first to meet the Indians in the spring. And so the two sets of traders leapfrogged up the North Saskatchewan, each trying to out-manoeuvre the other, each spurring the other deeper into the western territory.

The competitors faced each other across the river or wintered side by side in the shelter of the steep coulees. Sometimes relations were civil, but often they flared into drunken violence which disrupted the trade and scared off the Indians. The Canadians were bold, capable traders but they could also be half-literate, insensitive, violent men whose way of doing business was to mix equal quantities of liquor and abuse. There were many cases recorded of Indians being mistreated and having their furs stolen; the worst of the pedlars could never winter in the same place twice for fear of reprisals. In December 1778, up the North Saskatche-wan beyond the present site of Prince Albert, there were about a hundred and twenty Canadians wintering. Gathered on the ice in a milling mob, the pedlars opened a ten-gallon cask of rum, and a witness reported that when Indians arrived with furs "they made the Men Drink with them, and Seized on all their Horses and goods, and guarded them in and Locked them up within their Stockades." When the neighbouring Hudson's Bay Company trader objected, one of his men was beaten, and the French *voyageurs* muttered further threats against the English. The situa-tion was tense with suppressed hatred, and the following April the Indians struck back.

At a small outpost farther up the river a group of Cree shot and killed an independent trader, John Cole, who by all reports was notorious for his mistreatment of the Indians. Accounts of the incident are garbled, but the Indians seem to have allowed the rest of the people at the post to leave unharmed. The Canadians blamed their Hudson's Bay Company rivals for inciting the In-dians, and for a while a pitched battle threatened; but the Com-pany men scurried back to Cumberland House and tempers cooled. Nevertheless, for the next few seasons, trading on the Saskatchewan took place in an atmosphere of suspicion and fear.

The rivalry between the traders was much less devastating to the Indians, however, than the scourge which struck them in the fall of 1781. Traders first heard about it in October from an Indian man who told of a tent on the plains with seven people lying dead inside covered with the familiar red sores of smallpox. Within two weeks William Walker reported from up the river that "the Small pox is raging with such great Violence over the Country, not hardly sparing any that takes it. . . ." Men, women, and children were cut down in their tents or as they walked the trails to the trading posts. Their relations were afraid to touch them, and the sick and dying were left without food or water and, afterwards, without burial. Walker described "the Indians lying dead about the Barren Ground like Rotten Sheep, their Tents left standing and the Wild Beasts devouring them." The disease apparently was picked up from the Snake Indians in the Mississippi country and spread across the plains like a prairie fire. Before it had spent itself the epidemic carried off an estimated three-fifths of the native population of the West, an astounding figure which speaks of untold tragedy and hardship for the Indians. Unhappily it was just one of a series of similar epidemics brought by Europeans to the New World which eventually depleted the native population to a fraction of its original size.

Of all the pedlars it was perhaps Peter Pond, a fractious, restless trader from Connecticut, who made the deepest impression on the history of the West. Most of the independent Canadians spent a few years in the fur trade, then retired with their fortunes into obscurity. Pond aggressively sought out new regions of the country to exploit, opening up new transportation routes and forcing changes in the organization of the trade which eventually resulted in the creation of a single, united partnership of Canadian traders.

Peter Pond was born in New England in 1740, the son of a shoemaker. Apprenticed to the same trade, he joined the army instead because, as he later wrote, "I found tareing at home was too inactive a life for me. . . ." The young recruit took part in the never-ending series of border skirmishes between the French and New England colonies, and in 1760 he was with General Amherst for the attack on Montreal which ended French resistance on the St. Lawrence. At age twenty, Pond retired from the army a seasoned veteran. After a year at sea, he settled down in his home town of Milford, Connecticut, married, and began to raise a family. Later he recalled this brief pause in his wanderings as "the ondley three years of my life I was three years in one place since I was sixteen years old up to sixtey." (Apparently Pond did not use the time to learn how to spell.) His father was engaged in the fur trade at Detroit and Pond decided to give it a try, finding at last a way of life which suited his unsettled temperament. After six years in the Detroit country he shot a man in a duel and had to leave the trade temporarily. When he returned he shifted his headquarters to Michilimackinac, trading into the Mississippi country each winter. Finally, in 1775, he made his first trip beyond Lake Superior to the Northwest.

By the time Peter Pond arrived in the Saskatchewan country the Hudson's Bay Company had established Cumberland House and competition on the river was in full swing. As he crossed Lake Winnipeg that August he fell in with Alexander Henry, a fellow New Englander, who commanded four canoes of trade goods. A few days later they were joined by Thomas and Joseph Frobisher with six canoes. In all, thirty-seven canoes and close to two hundred men wintered in the Northwest that season. Henry and the Frobishers settled north of Cumberland House on Beaver Lake while the majority of the pedlars spread themselves along the shores of the Saskatchewan. Pond took his canoes south to Lake Dauphin, but in subsequent seasons he journeyed up the Saskatchewan with the rest until competition there made him start thinking about tapping the virgin territory farther to the north.

Actually it was the Frobisher brothers who blazed the trail which Pond would follow. Realizing that Chipewyan Indians from the Athabasca country brought their furs down the Churchill River each summer, either to Hudson Bay or Cumberland House, the Frobishers camped across their path and collected the trade as the Indians passed by. Furs from Athabasca grew thick and dark in the long cold winters and the brothers were anxious to penetrate up the river to the source of this rich trade. In 1776 Thomas got as far as Ile-à-la-Crosse where he was forced to stop for the winter and so the route at least this far was known when Pond's turn came two years later.

For several years pedlars in the West had been forming informal partnerships, pooling their goods to cut down on the incessant competition which disrupted the trade. Pond was backed by one of these groups when he set off up the Churchill with three canoes in the summer of 1778. No record of this expedition has survived. We know only that Pond and his men made it. Struggling against the current and led by Indian guides, they must have passed Frobisher's point of advance at Ile-à-la-Crosse, paddled up the La Loche River, crossed the lake of the same name, and come up against the height of land at the famous Methye Portage. As far as the fur traders were concerned, Methye was the top of the world. Behind them they left the familiar pathways of the Churchill and the Saskatchewan and the northern plains. Ahead lay the forests of the Athabasca country, the Mackenzie River basin, and, ultimately, the frozen shores of the Arctic Ocean. The portage itself was nineteen kilometres long and fairly level save for a precipitous drop of 210 metres to the Clearwater River at the north end. In the years ahead this rough footpath would be worn smooth by the heavy tread of thousands of *voyageurs* carrying their loads out of the Athabasca, but Pond was the first white man to cross this land bridge. Once across, everything he did was a first; he had come where no trader or explorer had been before. Leaving the Clearwater, he followed the Athabasca River to a point about sixty kilometres above Lake Athabasca, and there on the riverbank he erected a shelter and settled in for the winter.

Back on the Saskatchewan, as winter moderated into spring, Pond's partners waited anxiously. Rumours flew from log hut to log hut. "Some think he has starved for want of provisions," reported the surveyor Philip Turnor, "others think he is gone to far into the Country for them to receive any intelligence of him. . . ." Finally, on July 2, Pond's gang arrived back at Cumberland House. He had met with great success in his spring trading and had collected 140 packs of the finest furs. "He had Traded the Cloaths of his back," remarked another Hudson's Bay Company man enviously, "the Indians are so distressed and eager for Europeans Goods." The Athabasca country was now part of the fur traders' domain and with repeated visits its true value became clearer. Lake Athabasca lies at the hub of several major river systems. Northward to the Arctic flows the Slave and then the mighty Mackenzie. From the south, the Athabasca drains the wooded beaver country of northern Alberta. From the west, the Peace River brought trade from the Rocky Mountains over 1600 kilometres away. And eastward the Fond du Lac River connects through an arch of lakes back to the Churchill. At Athabasca, traffic following these different routes from the Rockies, the southern plains, and the Arctic tundra intersected. Not only that, but at its southwestern end was a watery delta, six thousand square kilometres in extent, which produced some of the richest furs to come out of the Northwest. Pond's expedition had opened up a veritable Eldorado.

Expansion brought problems as well as profits. A trader could only venture as far as his supplies could follow, and the logistics of the trade were becoming more and more complex. Athabasca was forty-four hundred kilometres from Montreal, and on the Saskatchewan pedlars were creeping farther west, away from their source of supply. Independent traders had often formed loose alliances lasting a season or more, but as the expansion of the trade required increased organization for shipping goods and provisioning the men, the virtues of some sort of permanent partnership became apparent.

The same year that Pond arrived back from Athabasca, eight separate alliances of Canadian traders and merchants agreed to form a single partnership. This has been called the first North West Company. Sixteen shares in the "company" were issued, each of the original alliances holding two. Veteran winterers such as the Frobishers, Charles Patterson, John Ross, and Robert Grant, along with substantial Montreal merchants such as the McGill brothers, Isaac Todd, Forrest Oakes, and the eventual "Marquis" of the western trade, Simon McTavish, were members of these groups. In practice it meant that instead of competing with each other these traders could pool their capital, spread themselves evenly through the fur country, and split their returns. A few years later several of the early partners withdrew to concentrate on the southwestern trade, and the original association was replaced by a new agreement naming eight shareholders, Peter Pond among them. But despite its shifting composition, the emergence of the North West Company marked a new phase in the Canadian trade — independent pedlars were giving way to organized partnerships.

The North West Company did not immediately succeed in monopolizing the fur business out of Montreal. There were just too many independent traders. For several years competition was intense as the Nor'westers slowly cornered the Canadian trade, and smaller partnerships struggled to keep a share of the market. As usual, Peter Pond was at the centre of the action. The Athabasca area, where Pond was now concentrating his abundant energies, was especially prized and the rivalry there was especially heated. Pond was an imperious and arrogant trader who tried to earn the fear, not the friendship, of the Indians. On one occasion a witness saw him strike a Chipewyan man with the flat of a sword and when his victim complained at such rough treatment Pond told him that "the country and the Indians belonged to him and he would do with them as he pleased. . . ." Pond dealt with his rival traders in the same manner. During the winter of 1781-82 he was opposed by the Swiss-born pedlar Jean-Etienne Waddens. One of Waddens' men, Joseph Faignant, later declared that one night he was in his room when he heard two shots fired in Waddens' room next door. Hurrying outside he saw Pond and a *voyageur* leaving Waddens' apartment, where he found his boss lying beside his bed with a gunshot wound in the leg. Waddens lost consciousness and died without naming his assailant, but Faignant also reported that Pond and the Swiss had been arguing heatedly earlier that evening. News of the killing spread quickly through the woods but there was really nobody to investigate or lay charges, and three years passed before authorities in Canada agreed, at the insistence of Waddens' widow, to take Pond into custody. He was examined, but nothing came of it, and he returned to the Northwest.

Pond seemed to attract trouble. In the winter of 1786-87 he was again involved in the murder of a rival trader, although this time he may not have been directly responsible. In his customary high-handed manner Pond was stripping some Chipewyans of their furs when his competitor, John Ross, interfered. A scuffle took place, Ross was fatally shot, and one of Pond's men, later described as "a little crack-brained and variable as the wind," slunk off into the woods, not to be seen in the outside world for three years. Again there was no hard evidence pointing in Pond's direction, and he was never charged. Three years later he retired from the trade back to his home in Connecticut.

Peter Pond's reputation has taken a beating because of these incidents and the testimony of his fellow traders. Alexander Mackenzie, who succeeded him in Athabasca, was the first of many to play up his ruthlessness and play down his solid contributions to the trade. In a half-hearted attempt at fairness, the surveyor David Thompson said of him: "He was a person of industrious habits, a good common education, but of a violent temper and unprincipled character." The economic historian, Harold Innis, rescued Pond from the rogue's gallery by emphasizing his pioneering mission into Athabasca and the part he played in solving transportation problems created by this expansion. As it turned out, even the murders in which Pond was implicated had an impact on the shape of the trade. By raising the spectre of a lawless frontier with traders gunning for each other in quest of furs, the murders helped to convince the different trading interests to abandon their rivalry.

In 1787 the North West Company absorbed its main competitor and gained unchallenged control of the Canadian trade. Now it could freely concentrate on outflanking its most formidable foe in the West, the Hudson's Bay Company.

CHAPTER THREE

Traders and Indians

The rivalry between the North West Company and the Hudson's Bay Company for control of the western fur country was as old as La Vérendrye and the French *coureurs*. Peter Pond, Samuel Hearne, and the others were following the tracks laid down by generations of traders before them. The problems they encountered were the same problems of distance and diplomacy encountered by Anthony Henday and Legardeur de Saint-Pierre. Their solutions were unique but they grew out of experience in the Indian trade and a growing knowledge of the contours of the western interior. Indeed, the rivalry was not really between two commercial enterprises at all; rather it was a rivalry between two great geographic possibilities. Would the resources of the western hinterland flow southeastward across the Great Lakes and down the Ottawa River to Canada? Or would they take the shorter route north and east through the stunted forest of the Shield to the swampy shores of Hudson Bay? For almost half a century the answer hung in the balance.

A glance at the map would suggest that the Hudson Bay route made the most sense. After all, the Bay was over two thousand kilometres closer to the best fur country and well connected by navigable waterways to the main arteries of the western trade. Yet the map is deceiving. It does not indicate the pride of a trading tradition, the ambitions of a rising commercial class, the enterprise of a group of traders linked by family ties and dreams of personal wealth. Nor does it show the more prosaic facts: the unequal distribution of the valuable birch tree or the maddening tendency of the British armed forces to conscript manpower which otherwise might have ended up in the employ of the Hudson's Bay Company. And so traders from Canada were able to corner an increasing share of the western furs despite the distances they had to travel. With the creation of the North West Company, the Canadian trading system reached its peak and the struggle for the fur empire was joined in earnest.

The Hudson's Bay Company and the North West Company both dealt in furs but they were as different as two trading companies possibly could be. They were organized differently; their employees were drawn from different places; they approached the native people differently; for the most part they even spoke different languages. The Hudson's Bay Company was in the traditional mould of the imperial trading company, chartered by the British monarch and given a monopoly to exploit the resources of its far-flung possessions. Headquartered in London, it was directed by men who had almost no first-hand knowledge of the fur trade. As a result they were cautious, even timid, and as the pressure of competition grew they were sometimes slow to grasp an opportunity or take a bold initiative. The Company drew its men at first from the English working class and increasingly from the Scottish islands. These men were called "servants" and the term suggests the deference employees were expected to show their "officers." Chances of promotion into the top ranks were slight, and there was little incentive for men to exert themselves unduly on the Company's behalf. But if the Hudson's Bay Company was at times sluggish, it was never inert. Rigor mortis was not setting in. When it embarked in new directions the Company moved forward relentlessly, and all its advantages of organization and experience made it a formidable competitor.

On the other hand the North West Company was a restive partnership of aggressive colonial merchants. Far from being cumbersome like its opponent, the Canadian concern was flexible and ever-changing as different partners joined and fell away. Most of its leading lights cut their teeth on the western trade and knew every aspect of the business. The upper ranks of the Company, the Nor'westers proper, were recruited primarily in Scotland and England. After serving in the "Indian country" as clerks, they could graduate to a full partnership in the Company, sharing materially in its profits and psychologically in its triumphs over all competitors. So many of these men were related to each other that it seemed that the old "Marquis," Simon McTavish, who directed the company until his death in 1804, was presiding over a family affair. The McGillivray brothers, one of whom, William, succeeded McTavish as chief, were all his nephews. Alexander Mackenzie was a cousin to Roderic Mackenzie who was the brother-in-law of McTavish's wife. Angus Shaw, a prominent western trader for many years, was a nephew-in-law; Simon Fraser was a cousin; David Thompson was a brother-in-law to a nephew; and so it went. The result was a degree of enthusiasm and enterprise that, for a time, completely dominated the western fur trade.

The lower ranks of the North West Company were filled by the French-Canadian *voyageurs* who paddled the canoes, hauled supplies, built the posts, and generally did the scut work. With few exceptions, they never became partners in the Company, remaining instead an unruly mob of salaried employees. *Voyageurs* have become the romantic figures of the trade, so much more colourful then the dour Scots who worked for the Hudson's Bay Company. We see them in our school books, dressed in their bright costumes and fearlessly shooting the foaming rapids with a song on their lips. (A collection of these songs, by the way, was once deemed unfit for publication because they were so obscene.) But the reverse side of their independence and pride was a tendency to resist the authority of their employer, and a North West Company post was often riven by squabbling between French *voyageurs* and English *bourgeois*. If a Hudson's Bay Company trading house resembled a military barracks, a Nor'wester establishment had more in common with a rowdy tavern.

Unlike the monolithic Hudson's Bay Company, the North West Company had a kind of split personality. In Montreal the merchant partners looked after marketing the furs and importing the mountain of goods which fueled the trade. Each winter they supervised the packing of ironware, guns, kegs of powder and bags of lead shot, tobacco, woollens and linens, blankets, and liquor. As well they hired the guides, interpreters, clerks, and paddlers who went with the canoes to the interior. At the other end of the system, in the interior, "wintering" partners supervised trading in the various districts. The conduct of business was in their hands. They sought out distant Indian groups; they developed new transport routes; they even altered the prices being offered for furs. Competition made such flexibility necessary. When opponents were settled nearby, prices could be lowered and bribes of liquor and tobacco handed out freely; when the field was clear, partners could drive a harder bargain. The ability to react quickly to changes in the local situation was a big advantage for the North West Company.

Every summer the two ends of the North West Company's operations converged on the hinge of the Canadian trade, the depot at Grand Portage at the head of Lake Superior. (After 1801 the depot moved to Fort William, sixty kilometres to the north.) This fourteen-kilometre portage, separating the Pigeon River from Lake Superior, also separated the relatively unobstructed navigation of the Great Lakes from the swifter, shallower waterways of the interior. As well, the Grand Portage separated two ways of life; the itinerant, unsupervised, violent, elemental life of the Northwest and the more genteel society of the St. Lawrence settlements. The Northmen best expressed this sense of crossing over into a different world. They were the *voyageurs* who manned the canoes from the interior, and for several years at a stretch they would not go east of the portage. A mystique, fed by their own boasting, grew up around the exploits of these inland travellers, and they loudly proclaimed their contempt for the soft life of their Montreal brothers. To keep the peace at Grand Portage, the two groups tented in separate camps divided by a small stream.

But business, not bragging, was the purpose of the annual rendezvous. Furs and supplies had to be carried across the portage and a partner up from Montreal brought news of the fur auctions, the activities of the competition and plans being made at head-quarters. Alexander Mackenzie described how "the proprietors, clerks, guides and interpreters, mess together, to a number of sometimes an hundred, at several tables, in one large hall, the provision consisting of bread, salt pork, tea, spirits, wine, etc. and plenty of milk, for which purpose several milch cows are constantly kept." Canoemen, however, kept to their own tents and their usual diet of boiled corn and fat. Once the goods had been trans-shipped and business matters attended to, a banquet and dance was held in the main hall at the post, and then the canoes hurried off east and west to make their destinations before the ice began to form.

From Montreal the trip had been made in the giant *canots du maîtres*, eleven metres long, propelled by eight to ten *voyageurs*, but at Grand Portage, travellers switched to the smaller North canoes, about seven metres in length and manned by a crew of four or five. The inland brigades made their arduous way through the country of the border lakes and down the Winnipeg River to the open waters of Lake Winnipeg. Along the way *voyageurs* fed on the familiar stew of boiled corn or wild rice flavoured with pork fat, but at Lake Winnipeg canoes were stocked with bags of pemmican, a mixture of powdered buffalo meat and fat which had become the staple item in a western traveller's diet. Pemmican was traded from the Plains Indians and stockpiled at key provisioning posts along the main transport routes. It provided a concentrated yet nutritious food supply which travelled well and did not spoil. Quite simply, the fur trade would have been impossible without it. As much as twenty thousand kilograms of pemmican were gathered along the Saskatchewan River alone each spring simply to feed the brigades moving up the river and north to Athabasca. During the winter buffalo meat continued to feed the people at the trading posts and a single post might consume a couple of hundred kilograms every day. As rival posts proliferated across the West, it is safe to assume that several million kilograms of pemmican were consumed in the fur country each year.

At Lake Winnipeg the brigades veered off toward their different destinations. Some canoes swung south into the Red River, continuing past the forty-ninth parallel or turning west up the Assiniboine to the posts which encroached on the southern plains. Others travelled up Lake Winnipeg, then hived off through a network of lakes and portages to the Swan River district. The Saskatchewan brigade continued northward to the top of Lake Winnipeg where it entered the mouth of the great river via the Grand Rapids and Cedar Lake. By now the Nor'westers would have crossed paths with some Hudson's Bay Company canoes which came inland from York Fort up the Hayes and Nelson rivers. York Fort was to the Hudson's Bay Company trading system what Grand Portage was to the Nor'westers. Like the mouth of a funnel, York sat at the outlet of a vast network of Indian canoe routes leading from the northern forest and the southern plains. Each summer, ships from Europe unloaded their supplies at this depot and collected the fur packs which had been brought from the interior. At times York controlled the trade of a hinterland which encompassed most of what today are the three prairie provinces and a large part of the Northwest Territories. Yet despite the size of the empire at its back, York Fort was a wretched place. "Nine months of winter varied by three of rain and mosquitoes," grumbled one unhappy resident. The post was set back from the bank of the Hayes River about ten kilometres inland from the shores of Hudson Bay. It looked out across a dismal landscape of bog and stunted forest with trees so small a grown man could see over them. In the winter there was no escaping the cold; the snow drifted as high as the roof eaves, and ice actually formed on the inside walls of the log dwellings. In the summer came oppressive heat and voracious mosquitoes which filled the nose and screamed in the ear. In the fall cold fogs rolled in off the Bay, and in the spring the ground was such a quagmire of mud that buildings had to be perched on pilings and everyone went about on board sidewalks. York Fort? "The very name gives me Colick," wrote one trader, "and the worst news I could now receive would be that I was again to winter there."

As the inland brigades toiled westward up the Saskatchewan, the low, marshy shoreline gradually gave way to higher, wooded banks edged here and there by a beach of sand and rock. Not long after passing Cumberland House the brigades entered the "tracking ground" where the current picked up speed and the river was broken by a series of rapids. Amid much grumbling, *voyageurs* spilled onto the shore and for several days tracked their loaded canoes upriver by hauling on long ropes. The heat was stifling and the hunched, sweating bodies of the men were enveloped in clouds of mosquitoes. Stumbling on the slippery rocks, sinking thigh deep into the mud and sand, the *voyageurs* struggled against the brown current from sunup to sundown. "This part of the River is an object of terror to the whole band," allowed the inland trader Duncan McGillivray.

Near the present site of Prince Albert, Saskatchewan, the brigade reached level ground, the current slackened, and with relief the men re-embarked in their canoes. Now the open prairie was coming into view. "The face of the Country here assumes a different appearance," wrote McGillivray, "hitherto our way has been obstructed by thick woods, on each side of the River but now extensive plains interspersed with only a few tufts of wood, open themselves to view, and extend to the utmost extremity of your sight round the Horizon, which appears as plain as in the midst of the Ocean in a perfect calm." Mosquitoes became less troublesome, but were replaced by a fine sand which blew off the steep banks into the eyes of the paddlers. The river followed a confused path through a labyrinth of sandbanks and willow islands and only the most experienced guide could keep the brigade from wandering into false channels and dead ends. The high banks were scarred with paths worn smooth by the buffalo which migrated across the river in huge herds. Running headlong over the escarpment down into the water, the animals were mindless of human intruders, and *voyageurs* who could not fend them off with paddles were swamped. At a spot on the river called *La Montée*, later the site of Fort Carlton, a few members of the brigade exchanged their canoes for horses traded from the Indians. Ranging across the grasslands, these outriders brought in a daily ration of freshly butchered meat to feed the *voyageurs* on the last leg of their exhausting voyage.

The north branch of the Saskatchewan River marked the

approximate boundary between wooded country to the north and grassland prairie to the south. Posts along its banks were strategically situated to gather furs from the Cree who inhabited the woods, while at the same time trading buffalo meat and horses from the Indians who inhabited the beaver-poor plains. Driven by a restless ambition, rival traders chased each other westward up the river, pausing every now and again to put up a draughty habitation before moving on, until the entire length of the waterway from Lake Winnipeg to the Rockies was dotted with posts like beads on a string. Similarly, major rivers like the Assiniboine, the Qu'Appelle, the Swan, and the Red were thickly inhabited by trading establishments. In fact, most rivers which provided a navigable canoe route and access to profitable hunting grounds were eventually settled by the ubiquitous traders, who, by the turn of the century, were drawing goods from every Indian group east of the mountains.

Trading posts were erected by the men themselves, so they had to be simply constructed and made of materials found on site. Buildings were set in a cleared quadrangle beside the river. In the middle stood the "main house," often a two-storey structure, made of logs plastered with mud and whitewashed. Inside, space was divided between a trading room and living quarters for the senior men. Floors were made of planks, and rooms were heated with stone fireplaces. Furniture was primitive. Other buildings were ranged along the sides of the quadrangle and contained the men's quarters, workshops, and storerooms. The entire establishment was enclosed by a stockade of pointed logs with bastions in opposite corners and gates opening in two directions. Outside the stockade there was sometimes a vegetable garden, a corral for the livestock, and the "plantation" where the Indians pitched their tents when they arrived to trade.

The actual trade was surrounded by a formal ritual that varied little from post to post whether the traders were from Canada or Hudson Bay. Indians were not shoppers in the modern sense. They visited the posts not only to obtain goods but also to indulge their love of ceremony, to renew friendships, and to emphasize their position of equality with the white strangers. Duncan McGillivray described the trading procedure which evolved.

> When a Band of Indians approach near the Fort it is customary for the Chiefs to send a few young men before them to announce their arrival, and to procure a few articles which they are accustomed to receive on these occasions — such as Powder, a piece of Tobacco and a little paint to besmear their faces, an operation which they seldom fail to perform previous to their presenting themselves before the *White People*. At a few yards distance from the gate they salute us with several discharges of their guns, which is answered by hoisting a flag and firing a few guns. On entering the house they are disarmed, treated with a few drams and a bit of tobacco, and after the pipe has been plyed about for some time they relate the news with great deliberation and ceremony. . . . When their lodges are erected by the women they receive a present of Rum proportioned to the Nation and quality of their Chiefs and the whole Band drink during 24 hours and sometimes much longer for nothing. . . . When the drinking match has subsided they begin to trade.

Traders honoured leaders of the bands by dressing them in scarlet coats, trousers, laced hats with coloured feathers, and linen shirts, and by giving them extra presents of tobacco and liquor. By giving a boost to a leader's authority, traders hoped to increase his prestige among his people which would in turn increase the amount of trade he brought to the post. Since rival companies indulged in gift-giving, it was not long before, in the words of one Nor'wester, "every man who killed a few skins was considered a chief and treated accordingly; there was scarcely a common buck to be seen, all wore scarlet coats. . . ."

The fur trade had no use for money. It was a barter trade, goods exchanged for goods. Still, a recognized standard of value had to be set if any business was going to be done. Therefore the beaver pelt became the accepted unit of "currency." A single prime pelt was called a *Made Beaver*, and all other items were measured against it. For instance, a gun might be worth fourteen Made Beaver, a blanket seven Made Beaver, a hatchet one Made Beaver, and so on. Many other types of pelts were traded and they were given an equivalent value in beaver skins — a marten equalled half a beaver, an otter one beaver, a bear three beaver. The result was that the total value of an Indian's furs could be given a Made Beaver value and theoretically he could then get an equivalent value in trade goods. Yet it is misleading to know these prices because they were seldom adhered to. The trade was too competitive and changeable for a fixed price list. In practise the standard was a minimum, and each trader worked to increase his take by means both fair and larcenous. First of all, he could arbitrarily raise prices, a move that did not please the Indians, who usually knew the old price, and that therefore wasn't very successful when competitors lived nearby. Secondly, he could haggle over the quality of the furs, claiming they were too worn, too small or too thin to bring full value. Thirdly, he could simply cheat the Indians by putting his thumb on the scale when weighing out shot, by using a short rule when measuring cloth, by diluting the brandy with water, and by substituting second-hand or second-rate goods for the top of the line. Cheating was so common that it was an accepted part of the trade. Profits made from it were entered on the account books and the Indians themselves knew how the traders operated. "You told me last year to bring many Indians to trade, which I promised to do," announced one leader,

> you see I have not lied; here are a great many young men come with me; use them kindly, I say; let them trade good goods I say! We lived hard last winter and hungry, the powder being short measure and bad; being short measure and bad, I say! Tell your servants to fill the measure, and not to put their thumbs within the brim. . . . The guns are bad, let us trade light guns, small in the hand, and well shaped, with locks that will not freeze in the winter, and red gun cases. . . . Give us good measure of cloth; let us see the old measure; do you mind me?

"Give us good measure," the Indians said, asking for fair treatment. Yet the traders continued to charge what the market would bear. After all, they reasoned, the Indians were given no end of presents every time they visited the post, so why not balance the books with a little overcharging? Furthermore, since the Indians did not like to see prices changing every year, the value of their furs could not fluctuate with prices in the European market. Neither could the traders refuse to take furs in periods of glut. In other words, the conventional economics of supply and demand did not apply. As a result, traders used informal methods of compensating for a relatively inflexible price system.

The Indians were not defenceless when it came to trading. They were as expert at haggling as the white man, and they could simply refuse to trade their furs if they couldn't strike a deal. This threat was given special force when rival traders were in business nearby. Then the Indian with his furs had a choice and could play one against the other to get a better price for his goods. Neither were the Indians averse to practising some petty larceny of their own. Credit was an important part of the trading system and had been almost from the beginning. Indians were "trusted" with a quantity of goods in the fall on the understanding that they would repay their debt in the spring when they had trapped some furs. Yet the Indians sometimes refused to pay up, pleading poverty or sickness, and if a trader pressed the issue the debtor could simply decamp for another post where he might start with a clean slate. In theory credit seemed very much in the trader's interest. What better way of controlling Indian behaviour than by keeping him in debt to the Company? But in practise the Indians did not always recognize these economic obligations and refused to be kept under the trader's thumb.

What all of this makes clear is that the fur trade was a unique economic system. It was not a system invented by merchants in the Old World and imposed on the New. Instead it evolved out of conditions in the North West and the cultural needs of the people who lived there. A shopkeeper in Montreal or London would have been bewildered if he had been expected to treat his customers to a smoke and a drink, sit through a long speech in which he was alternately beseeched and berated, and then dress them in fine clothes so they would be sure to bring him their business next time. But gift-giving and oration were very much a part of Indian "commerce" and so they became part of the fur trade. The trade was carried on according to certain rules, which were systematically broken. At first glance the whole enterprise seems farcical. There was a price standard which was ignored, debts which were not repaid, and cheating which was openly declared. But each of these elements was part of the compromise between Indian and European trader which characterized the trade. Elements of farce are perhaps inevitable when economies and cultures as different as these meet and attempt to do business.

Although Canadians and Europeans came into the West to collect furs, the actual trading period only occupied a few days in the spring and fall. In summer, traders were on the move between their inland posts and the depots at Grand Portage and Hudson Bay. The rest of the time was marked by monotony rather than the high adventure we have come to associate with the fur trade. The men subsisted on fish and wild game, and most of their time was taken up with hunting and fishing. Still, a great deal of their food was bartered from the Indians; without this supply of buffalo and moose meat the newcomers would have starved. When they weren't out hunting, they were gathering wood to feed their insatiable fires or patching up the dilapidated houses. But through the dark, cold days of winter there was much free time for gambling, reading, writing letters, and brooding on distant places and half-forgotten friends. It was a time an active trader hated, a time of depression and lethargy, broken by nervous outbursts of violence and drunkenness.

Life at a Hudson's Bay Company post differed from life at a North West Company establishment. The English company expected its men to be obedient and sober. Early in its history the Company had recruited from among the labouring classes of the large British cities but these men were thought to be unsuitable because they were "acquainted with the ways and debaucheries of the town." Instead, an apprenticeship system was introduced. Young boys, sometimes only twelve years old, were taken from orphanages and charity schools and bound to the Company's service for up to seven years. They received a small salary and a chance to learn the skills of the trade, and when their term ran out many signed on as regular servants. The result was a pool of "Company men," experienced, disciplined, and obedient. Early in the eighteenth century the Company began to recruit its labourers from the Orkney Islands. These men, raised on the marginal farms and in the fishing villages of the rocky islands, were used to working hard for not much reward, and were able to endure much without complaint. Scots "are a hardy people both to endure hunger, and cold, and are subject to obedience," said an early Hudson's Bay Company governor. No wonder they appealed to a company looking for tractable employees. For their part, the Orkneymen were attracted to the fur trade by the chance to earn good wages and by a thirst for adventure. Orkneymen fulfilled the expectations held for them. Fathers brought in their sons and brothers recruited brothers until by 1800 about three-quarters of the Hudson's Bay Company men were from the Islands. Many of these men later settled in the West and formed an important Scottish element in the unique society taking shape there.

A North West Company post was a much less disciplined place. The wintering partners were never able to assert the same degree of authority over their French-Canadian *voyageurs*. This was much in keeping with the less structured, more democratic organization of the Canadian company in general. There seems to have been no love lost between the English-speaking partners and clerks and the French canoemen. The former may have respected the latters' abilities with the paddle but they had little patience for them as wintering companions. "With a slight education, if any, and no books, when in their wintering houses they passed their time in card playing, gambling and dancing," reported David Thompson, "which brought on disputes, quarrels and all respect was lost. Goods beyond the extent of their wages were taken by the men to pay their gambling debts, and every festival of the church of Rome was an excuse to get drunk. . . ." This behaviour has become part of the *voyageurs'* colourful legend today, but many of the Nor'westers had only contempt for it. Daniel Harmon, with a party of *voyageurs,* came to the Swan River in 1800 to trade. He was the only Englishman in the group and there was not a soul at the post for him to talk to for weeks on end. He consoled himself with the thought that "what conversation would an illiterate ignorant Canadian be able to keep up. All of their chat is about Horses, Dogs, Canoes and Women, and strong Men who can fight a good battle." It was disingenuous of David Thompson to blame *voyageurs* for running up debts with the Company; the mark-up on goods from the Company stores was very high and it was well known that the *bourgeois* encouraged their men to go into debt as a way of keeping a hold over them. It is no wonder that the French were sometimes restless under the command of their high-minded, often priggish employers. It has been tempting for romantically-inclined historians to present the fur trade as an example of French and English working together to develop the resources of the continent, but if the fur trade is an example of anything it is of the uneasy relations between the two groups which have so often plagued the country.

While traders were absorbed by their business concerns, the Indians of the West went about their own lives in many ways unaffected by the presence of so many newcomers to their lands. The two groups met briefly at the posts to exchange goods, each receiving from the other things it could not produce for itself. Then they parted, the Indians returning to a world the trader never entered or understood, a world with its own patterns of trade, its own religion and social relations, its own wars and alliances. Traders from Canada and Europe obviously affected events in this world. They introduced new goods into it and disrupted its balance of power. But for the most part the traders were peripheral to the real concerns of the Indian people.

Until quite recently it was fashionable to emphasize the dependence of Indians on the traders. Native people quickly saw the superiority of European trade goods, such as ironware, cloth, and guns, abandoned their traditional ways of doing things, and fell headlong into an abject reliance on the trading post. At least that is how the argument goes, as if an entire civilization could be bought off with a kettle and a gun.

This interpretation is wrong for two reasons. First of all, it neglects to point out that traders were far more dependent on the Indians than vice versa. Aside from supplying furs, native people supplied most of the food without which the traders would have been forced to leave the country. As well, they helped transport goods, made snowshoes and canoes, and guided the newcomers through the bewildering maze of waterways to distant fur grounds. All of these chores were vital to the success of the fur trade. Nothing the traders offered in return, except perhaps guns, can be considered vital to the welfare of the Indians.

Secondly, to believe in the dependence of the Indians is to overlook the opinions of the traders themselves, who were always regretting their own lack of influence. Ever since Anthony Henday had visited the Blackfoot at mid-century, traders had complained that the western Indians would rather hunt buffalo, steal horses, and make war than produce furs for the white man. Duncan McGillivray summed up the situation from his post on the Saskatchewan. In his opinion, the Plains people lived "very happily independent of our assistance. They are surrounded with innumerable herds of various kinds of animals . . . and they have invented so many methods for the destruction of Animals, that they stand in no need of ammunition to provide a sufficiency for these purposes." McGillivray pointed out that the traders had only liquor, tobacco, and ammunition to attract the Indians. "The rest of our commodities are indeed useful to the Natives, when they can afford to purchase them, but if they had hitherto lived unacquainted with European productions it would not I believe diminish their felicity."

The impact of the trade was different for every Indian group. McGillivray was speaking about the Plains Indians who, because of their reliable food supply, could afford to be more independent of the traders than could their Woodland neighbours who specialized in hunting furs. Nonetheless, the fur trade did not destroy native culture. Indians were participants in the trade, not its victims. And they participated as independent people with a keen sense of their own needs, not as dupes who sold their birthright for a mess of beads and trinkets.

The traders from away did not bring any women with them into the West. The fur business was for men only. But this did not mean that they lived celibate lives. Indian women were numerous and it was a rare trader who did not have a "country wife" to share his lodgings. These relationships were far more than sexual affairs; they were as affectionate and durable as European-style marriages. Indeed, many liaisons led to marriage of a kind. According to the "custom of the country," borrowed from the native people, a trader took a wife by obtaining the permission of her parents and paying the "bride price" set by her relatives. These marriages *a la façon du pays* did not have the benefit of clergy but they were solemnized by Indian ritual and recognized as valid.

The Hudson's Bay Company feared these marriages and banned them, with little success. Its rival had a more pragmatic view. The Canadian partners knew from experience that, sex and romance aside, marriage was the best way to cement a trade alliance. If a trader wanted to be sure that an Indian leader brought his furs to the post each year, there was no better way than to marry his daughter. North West partners also were not above acting as pimps, stealing Indian women in payment for debts owed by fathers or husbands, "then selling them to their men [for] from five hundred to two thousand *livres* and if the Father or Husband or any of them resist the only satisfaction they get is a beating. . . ." However, force was not usually needed since the Indians saw the advantages of being linked by marriage to the strangers and frequently forced their women upon them.

Eventually the Hudson's Bay Company recognized the wisdom of country marriages and relaxed its restrictions, not only for reasons of trade but also because women were already proving valuable, if unofficial employees. "They clean and put into a state of preservation all Beavr. and Otter skins brought by the Indians undried and in bad Condition," explained a letter from the Bay in 1802. "They prepare Line for Snow shoes and knit them also without which your Honors servants could not give efficient opposition to the Canadian traders they make Leather shoes for the men who are obliged to travel about in search of Indians and furs and are useful in a variety of other instances, in short they are Virtually your Honors Servants and as such we hope you will Consider them." The result was that western fur trade posts were filled with children and all the confusion of family life.

Yet for all that Indians and traders intermarried and intermingled, relations between them were strained, marked by suspicion, and punctuated by outbursts of violence and murder. As the brigades moved slowly up the Saskatchewan River each season, they were watched over by armed men on horseback who patrolled the high banks on the lookout for Indian ambush. At more than one post, people lived in terror of their lives. Sometimes the problem was local, caused by the stupidity or brutality of an individual trader. This was the case in 1780 on the Saskatchewan when one of the pedlars, renowned for his double-dealing, was murdered by Indians and the whole trading community retreated down the river in fear of an uprising that never came. More basic was the system of Indian alliances which the newcomers did not understand. The traders bartered guns to some Indian groups which then used the new weapons to make war on their neighbours. Naturally enough, traders were then seen as allies of their trading partners, and as such became the enemies of their enemies. On the plains, for example, the Gros Ventres came to hate the people who supplied their Cree enemies with guns, and in the Red River area the Sioux from the south terrorized the posts frequented by their enemies, the Ojibwa. There is evidence in the traders' journals that plans were brewing in 1780 to drive the newcomers from the Northwest. The Plains Indians were not as interested in trading as their Woodland neighbours, and, according to John Macdonell, a Nor'wester in southern Manitoba, the Indians were developing plans "of cutting off all the white men in the interior country." It is possible that had the smallpox not swept the plains at this point, with drastic results for the native people, the fur trade in the West might have been brought to a violent close.

In the next decade the Gros Ventres took the offensive. "They are an audacious, turbulent race," thought Alexander Henry the

Younger, "and have repeatedly attempted to menace us." Their first move was to plunder a Hudson's Bay Company post on the North Saskatchewan. Then, in July 1794, the Gros Ventres attacked a North West Company post on the south branch of the river. The alarm was raised, however, and the post was securely locked. After exchanging gunfire for half an hour the warriors shifted their attention to a Hudson's Bay Company post not far away. They were able to take the small settlement totally by surprise, killing three men and five or six women and children before setting the buildings ablaze. One man managed to escape by hiding in a pile of rubbish, then scurrying under cover of smoke to a canoe and making his way downriver with news of the attack. However, this was the extent of the "uprising." The Gros Ventres withdrew, and though for several years rumours that they were coming again to attack the traders flew up and down the river, they eventually made their peace with the white men. The Indians were not united enough to drive the traders from the Northwest. And as time passed there appeared to be less and less reason to do so. Traders were too valuable to be evicted. The goods they imported were extremely useful to the Indians, both in peace and in war, and it would have been unlikely that the native people would destroy a trading system which served their interests.

As the century drew to a close the battle for the furs of the Northwest was going decidedly in the favour of the upstart company from Canada. In two decades the Nor'westers had come to control over seventy-eight per cent of the trade, leaving a paltry amount for their older rival the Hudson's Bay Company to share with the few independent traders still in the field. The British company was matching the Canadian post for post across the West, but there was no matching the ruthless energy of the Nor'westers. Hudson's Bay Company men carried on business on the Saskatchewan "as if it were drawn by a dead Horse," crowed their rivals. They were shorthanded, lacked drive, and feared the Indians. All of which led Duncan McGillivray to suggest that the venerable company should "adopt some terms of agreement" with the Nor'westers; in other words, throw in the towel.

However, it was a little early for surrender. McGillivray was a few years ahead of his time; there would be no union yet. Even as the Nor'westers seemed to be getting the best of the Bay Company, new competitors were getting ready in Montreal to join the struggle for the fur trade empire. These competitors were experienced, wealthy, and equal to the knock-about aggressiveness of the Nor'westers. As the new century opened, the old rivalry was put aside for a while to meet this formidable challenge.

CHAPTER FOUR

Two Caesars

In the summer of 1799 the partners and agents of the North West Company met as usual for their annual council at Grand Portage. For some time the amicability which marked these get-togethers had been soured by a growing resentment on the part of the winterers. For several years the Montreal end of the business had been centred in the offices of a single company, McTavish, Frobisher and Company, and the affairs of that company had been collecting in the hands of a single man, Simon McTavish. McTavish, Frobisher and Company acted as the principal agent for the North West Company, buying trade goods, selling furs, and forwarding supplies. The winterers grumbled at the way McTavish wielded power within the circle of partners and at the way shares were manoeuvred to keep control with himself and his allies. Four years before, the up-countrymen had balked at proposals for a new partnership agreement but rebellion fizzled out when the number of shares in the Company was increased, making room for new partners. Now, in 1799, the winterers were once again in a rebellious mood. And when Alexander Mackenzie, the man they took to be their spokesman and ally, rose from his seat at the council table to announce that he was withdrawing from McTavish, Frobisher, indeed, withdrawing from the fur trade altogether, his words struck the meeting like sparks into dry grass.

It is small wonder that the winterers found their spokesman in

Alexander Mackenzie. Unlike McTavish, a stranger to most of them, a man who had never even ventured west of Grand Portage, Mackenzie was an authentic Nor'wester, a ten-year veteran of the fur country who knew first-hand the perils of the Indian trade. He had been born in Stornoway, on the windswept northern Isle of Lewis, and as a young boy he had come to America with his widowed father to escape the stony soils and predatory landlords of his native Scotland. During the American Revolution Alexander's father fought and died on the royalist side. The youngster went to live with his aunts in the Mohawk Valley, but, as the fighting drew closer, he was bundled off to Montreal to go to school.

In 1779 the fifteen-year-old Mackenzie began work in the counting house belonging to John Gregory, a leading merchant in the fur trade. It was an exciting time to be getting an introduction to the fur business. As he worked in the Montreal warehouse, Mackenzie would have learned about Peter Pond's journey to the distant Athabasca country and the rivalry on the Saskatchewan which led to the creation of the first North West Company. Gregory and his partner Normand McLeod, for some reason, remained aloof from the new concern. Instead they recruited their own band of winterers, and, in 1785, Mackenzie was one of them, dispatched into the Northwest for the first time.

But competition proved costly and violent, and two years later Gregory gave up the fight. As a result of the deal that was negotiated, Alexander Mackenzie, twenty-three years old, became a shareholder in the North West Company.

Mackenzie's career here took a fortunate turn; he was sent to winter at a post on the Athabasca River with the legendary Peter Pond. Pond's career was drawing to a close, he would leave the fur country the next summer and never return, and he outlined to his young successor the ambitious plans for discovery he had made during his decade in Athabasca. Pond had probably travelled as far north as Great Slave Lake, and from the Indians he had collected enough information to round out his own confused geography of the northland. According to Pond, and he probably shared his theories with Mackenzie, a broad river rising in Great Slave Lake flowed westward across the continent and emptied into the Pacific Ocean. He believed that the Rocky Mountains, which obviously would interfere with this theory, ended at about latitude 62° north, allowing his river to flow without interruption to the sea. Not only was the route easily travelled, it would not take long since Pond also miscalculated the location of Lake Athabasca, placing it at least eleven hundred kilometres further west than it is and assuming it lay within an easy six-day paddle of the Pacific.

It fell to Mackenzie to carry out Pond's scheme. In the summer of 1789 he ventured north to Great Slave Lake and embarked upon the westward flowing river. Unfortunately, it soon began to turn northward instead, carrying Mackenzie and his party to the edge of an ice-shrouded sea which he knew could not possibly be the Pacific Ocean. In fact he had reached the Arctic Ocean, but being the first man to explore the Mackenzie River to its mouth was small consolation since the route was of little use to the fur trade. However, it did whet Mackenzie's appetite for exploration and in 1793 he set out again, up the Peace River this time, in search of a route to the "Western Sea." After crossing the Rockies, Mackenzie descended the Fraser River and with Indian help trudged overland to the Bella Coola River which led him at last to the shores of the Pacific.

As in the case of his first great voyage, Mackenzie's expedition to the Pacific matters more as a feat of overland exploration than as an important breakthrough for the fur trade. The actual route he travelled would never be an important trade route but it made his reputation as one of the most intrepid and audacious of all the trader-explorers.

For all his fame as a northern explorer, Mackenzie at times hated the fur trade and the north country. He was satisfied as long as he was active, but the long winters of harsh cold, idleness, and solitude did not suit his intense temperament. Just before setting off on his Pacific expedition, he wrote to his cousin Roderic that it was "the height of folly" to endure the fur trader's life, "deprived of every comfort that can render life agreeable." After his return he passed what appears to have been a gloomy winter at Fort Chipewyan, tormented by depression and terrifying dreams. "Though I am not superstitious," he confided to Roderic, "my dreams caused me much annoyance. I could scarcely close my eyes without finding myself in company with the dead. I had visions of late which almost convince me that I have lost a near relation or friend." It must have been a relieved Mackenzie who took his leave of the Athabasca country for the last time in the summer of 1794.

If Mackenzie found an isolated trading post boring and depressing, life in Montreal was much more congenial. Many traders who made comfortable fortunes in the Northwest retired to Quebec where they joined a small elite of opulent merchants and landed gentry. Some bought seigneuries in the country; others lived in stone mansions at the edge of town with orchards and wine cellars and ranks of servants. Mackenzie shared a house with his close friend William McGillivray, another bachelor trader, nephew to Simon McTavish, and, as quickly became evident, heir apparent to his uncle's throne. The two friends travelled together each summer to the rendezvous at Grand Portage to represent the Company, and in the winter months they amused themselves with a hectic round of dinners and parties and boozy meetings of the Beaver Club. One of their drinking companions, a visitor to Montreal named George Landmann, left a memorable description of one of these occasions.

> In those days we dined at four o'clock, and after taking a satisfactory quantity of wine, perhaps a bottle each, the married men . . . retired, leaving about a dozen to drink to their health. We now began in right earnest and true highland style, and by four o'clock in the morning, the whole of us had arrived at such a state of perfection, that we could all give the war-whoop as well as Mackenzie and McGillivray, we could all sing admirably, we could all drink like fishes, and we all thought we could dance on the table without disturbing a single decanter, glass or plate by which it was profusely covered; but on making the experiment we discovered that it was a complete delusion, and ultimately, we broke all the plates, glasses, bottles, etc., and the table also, and worse than

all the heads and hands of the party received many severe contusions, cuts and scratches.

The next spring Landmann accompanied his new friends on their annual trip west and he reported that at Lachine the party paused for lunch at a house belonging to the North West Company.

> We sat down, and without loss of time, expedited the lunch intended to supersede a dinner, during which time the bottle had freely circulated, raising the old Highland drinking propensity, so that there was no stopping it; Highland speeches and sayings, Highland reminiscences; and Highland farewells, with the dioch and dorich, over and over again, was kept up with extraordinary energy, so that by six or seven o'clock, I had, in common with many of the others fallen from my seat. To save my legs from being trampled on, I contrived to draw myself into the fire-place, and sat up in one of the corners there being no stove or grate.

From his position huddled in the fireplace, Landmann watched while one after another the diners fell drunkenly from their chairs until only Mackenzie and McGillivray remained at their places.

> Mackenzie now proposed to drink to our memory, and then give the war-whoop over us, fallen foes and friends, all nevertheless on the floor, and in attempting to push the bottle to McGillivray, at the opposite end of the table, he slid off his chair, and could not recover his seat whilst McGillivray, in extending himself over the table, in the hope of seizing the bottle which Mackenzie had attempted to push to him, also in like manner began to slide on one side, and fell helpless on the floor.

Mackenzie was a partner in McTavish, Frobisher and Company but his relations with McTavish, the senior partner, must have been strained in these years leading up to the fateful meeting of 1799. It was more than Mackenzie's readiness to speak up for the wintering partners. Ever since his expedition to the far ocean he had been mulling over the need for a fundamental reorientation of the Canadian trade. He believed that since the fur business had penetrated so deeply into the continent it would make more sense to ship furs westward across the Rockies and down to the Pacific where they could be taken for sale by ship to China. Furthermore, Mackenzie recognized that the shorter Hudson Bay route to the interior offered overwhelming advantages for shipping trade goods and supplies inland, and he suggested that the Canadian company come to an agreement with its rival. Such notions were a heresy to Simon McTavish. His business, his personal wealth and power, depended on the St. Lawrence trade and long-established ties to British fur markets. He could not be expected to endorse a scheme which threatened to destroy a business he had spent his entire career nurturing.

Simon McTavish was about fifteen years older than his junior partner Mackenzie. He also had come to America from Scotland as a boy, probably to apprentice with a merchant in New York. Details about McTavish's life are scanty, but by the 1770s he apparently was engaged in the fur trade out of Albany. In 1774 he moved to Montreal where, in partnership with James Bannerman, he got involved in the Northwest trade. McTavish was largely responsible for hammering out the agreements which eventually led to the formation of the North West Company and it was not long before his own firm controlled this loose amalgam of partnerships.

There were those who found McTavish an arrogant, autocratic man. Certainly he could not have dominated such a restive, ambitious group of merchants without being ruthless when the situation demanded it and for this he earned his nickname, "The Marquis." The fur business was not polite and McTavish must have been a bit of a pirate to succeed in it. Nevertheless, as a young man he was known as an inveterate sampler of "good wine, good oysters and pretty girls" and he had the same love of late nights and fine liquor as had the younger generation of Mackenzie and McGillivray. He was forty-three before he took a wife, seventeen-year-old Marie Marguerite Chaboillez, daughter of a veteran trader. He planned for her a huge stone mansion at the foot of the mountain, the largest of the "fur chateaux," suggesting that MacTavish shared the pride and ostentation of the colony's other merchant princes. Whatever his character, McTavish's accomplishments mark him as one of the most decisive and adroit business leaders in Canadian history, more than a match for the combative Mackenzie, as events would prove.

It is still unknown what circumstances, or combination of circumstances, led Mackenzie to withdraw from his old associates that summer of 1799. He may have been bluffing, hoping to win a better position in the company for himself and his supporters. But if he expected that McTavish would beg him to stay on he received a rude shock; he returned to Montreal ready to change his mind and "The Marquis" instead preferred to accept the resignation. This could only have worsened relations between the two men and undoubtedly fueled the bitter rivalry which would come later.

Alternatively, Mackenzie's withdrawal may have resulted from a momentary burst of temper which he afterwards regretted. This is the interpretation supported by the comments of John Fraser, McTavish's partner and agent in London, who spoke with Mackenzie that winter. According to Fraser, the resignation arose "entirely from a fit of ill-humour, without any fix'd plan. . . ." However, William McGillivray contradicted Fraser, writing that his friend had long planned to quit the trade. "He has realized a handsome Sum of Money and quits a very troublesome Business," concluded McGillivray, with perhaps a touch of envy. But what about McGillivray? Did Mackenzie perhaps resent his friend's rise to senior partnership in the McTavish firm and suspect that it was more a result of his uncle's sponsorship than merit? Certain documents came to light not long ago which hint that Mackenzie's behaviour at Grand Portage was part of a daring attempt to oust Simon McTavish and instal himself as "The Marquis" of the Canadian trade. Perhaps this is what Alexander Henry meant when he wrote about the incident to a friend: "as there could not be two Caesars in Rome one must remove."

Whatever the reasons — pride, ambition, jealousy — Mackenzie did resign from the company he had served for a dozen years and embarked for England, evidently in a high dudgeon. That winter he spent brooding in London, nursing his ill-humour and plotting revenge. John Fraser wrote to McTavish to warn him: ". . . you know him to be vindictive, he has got an entire ascendant over your young Men, and if driven to desperation he may take steps ruinous to you. He has told myself Your Nt. West business will be completely ruin'd; to others he has thrown out most violent threats of revenge, and I have had some hints too extravagant to mention."

Mackenzie's defection came at a particularly awkward time for McTavish and his partners. They were not the only traders working out of Montreal. While they controlled the trade beyond Lake Superior, other companies were doing business in the forests of the "Old Northwest," the vast territory to the south and west of the Great Lakes. Since the American War of Independence this land had belonged to the United States, but at first Americans did nothing to assert their claim, and trade went on much as always. As the century drew to a close, however, the United States became interested in the fur resources of its western territory and began to regulate access by foreign, i.e., Canadian, traders. Well-established companies in Montreal as a result abandoned the "southern trade" and began organizing to challenge North West Company hegemony in the West. Competition was not new to the Nor'westers. They had always had to deal with the Hudson's Bay Company and even the St. Lawrence trade was regularly contested. But over the years they had worked out their own ways of dealing with anyone bold or naïve enough to oppose them. Those rivals who were wealthy enough to pose a real threat were absorbed into the partnership; small fry who were too unimportant to absorb were driven forcibly from the country.

Take the case of Dominic Rousseau, a Montreal merchant of small means. He dispatched a canoe to Grand Portage one summer thinking that the Nor'westers at their rendezvous would provide a ready market for some of his goods. The enterprise was under the command of a man named Hervieu. Hervieu pitched his tent close by the company post and opened for business. But the North West Company preferred its men to buy things from its own stores, where prices could be "controlled." Duncan McGillivray paid Hervieu a visit and asked him to pack up his goods and clear off. Hervieu stood his ground, pointing out quite correctly that he had as much right to be there as anyone else. McGillivray's response was less legalistic. He returned with a gang of bullies, sliced the canvas with a knife, tore down the tent, scattering its contents about the ground, and warned Hervieu that if he didn't leave at once he would be beaten to a pulp. As a result of this incident Dominic Rousseau was awarded £500 damages by the courts in Lower Canada. A few years later he was emboldened to try again. This time he sent two canoes under a man named Delorme on an actual trading mission to the Indians. In order to avoid the Nor'westers, Delorme skirted the rendezvous, but as he was making his way through the border lakes country a party of company men overtook him. Instead of beating up Delorme, however, they forged on ahead and began to fell trees across the streams and portage trails he would have to follow. Delorme could make no progress and finally emptied his goods on the ground and went home. This time the North West Company offered to make amends by buying the abandoned outfit, at Montreal prices.

However, the opposition which emerged in the last few years of the century would not be chased from the Northwest with its tail between its legs; it was experienced, organized and well-financed. It was led by the Montreal firm of Forsyth, Richardson and Company, a partnership of two cousins, John Forsyth and John Richardson. Originally this firm was preoccupied with the "southern trade" to the United States, but the future of this business had become increasingly problematic since the Treaty of Versailles (1783) gave the southern fur country to the new republic. Americans did not assert their sovereignty at all vigorously, and because British troops continued to occupy the frontier forts, traders from Montreal continued to do business there. Jay's Treaty finally set a definite date (1796) for the evacuation of the forts by the British, and the handwriting was on the wall. Firms like Forsyth, Richardson reoriented their operations toward the Northwest, where the best furs were anyway, and where, of course, the field was already occupied.

In organizing its challenge to the North West Company, Forsyth, Richardson followed the precedent set by the "Old Concern" and made a co-partnership arrangement with several Canadian companies. The "New Concern" was known both as the New North West Company and the XY Company, apparently because its bales were stamped with an "XY" to identify them. By its rivals it was also called the "Little Company" in derision, and its men were "potties," probably a *Canadien* term referring to something of little worth. As the contest got under way the betting was all with the "Old Concern." "The New North West Company is going on," reported the elder Alexander Henry. "It will be a considerable struggle, but I know who will gain. The one party is a new raised corps without discipline. . . . I can't find one man of experience that has the least knowledge of the North concern'd."

The odds changed in the summer of 1800 when Alexander Mackenzie returned from London and threw in his lot with the challengers. The XY Company was thereafter often called simply "Alexander Mackenzie and Company" in recognition of the fact that it was his reputation which attracted the experienced hands and his animosity which gave the struggle its intensity.

Competition between the two Canadian companies lasted only six seasons, but they were six seasons well remembered for their violence, debauchery, and waste. Never before had a commercial rivalry come so close to open warfare. Prices were slashed, wages inflated, and the fur country was soaked in cheap rum. "No good can be derived from the turbulent struggles of opposition in this country," summarized Nor'wester W. F. Wentzel, "it destroys trade, creates vice, and renders more people crafty, ruins good morals, and almost totally abolishes human sentiment in both Christian and Indian breasts."

The struggle for furs often became hand-to-hand combat. Prices were manipulated, but if the Indians could not be bribed then they were bullied. As one trader put it, ". . . preventing the opposition from making returns is the Great Point and nothing must stand in its way." To this end rival traders spent a lot of time spying on each other to prevent trade from falling into the other's hands and to find out where the opposition was getting its furs.

"Keep all your men constantly running about among the Indians," read the instructions from XY headquarters, "to pick up whatever skins they can, and wherever your neighbours send to let some of yours follow them. . . ." Traders took to skulking about after dark or in bad weather in comic attempts to throw their opponents off the scent. One result of all this espionage was that large numbers of employees were required to man the posts, a fact which favoured the "Old Concern." Despite being equally well financed, the XYs could muster only about four hundred men to the North West Company's one thousand. Not that the labour market was allowed to work freely. Both sides raised wages, offered signing bonuses, and even hired more men that they needed just to keep seasoned hands from joining the opposition.

The Indians, naturally enough, took advantage of their position to extort more liberal treatment from the traders. "The Indians have lost all industry," complained one Nor'wester, "[they] are becoming careless about hunting and paying their credits, as they well know that when one will refuse, another more extravagant will readily give. They now get a quantity of things so easily that they have grown quite extravagant. . . ." Unhappily for the Indians there was not all that much they wanted from the traders and so they spent their wealth on liquor and tobacco, mostly liquor.

Booze had always been an important part of the fur trade and the Canadians had always handed out generous portions. A dozen years before, the Hudson's Bay Company's William Tomison had remarked: "The Canadians is going through the Barren Ground with Rum, like so many ravenous Wolves, seeking whom they may devour." But competition loosened whatever final inhibitions the traders might have had and liquor flowed into the Northwest in unprecedented quantities. From an estimated annual average of ninety-six hundred gallons of "rum and spirits" leaving Canada each season before 1799, the amount jumped to a total of twenty-one thousand gallons in 1803. Since liquor was generally mixed with four parts water, the Northwest was awash in more than a hundred thousand gallons of "that pernicious article, rum." Liquor became the currency of the country. It was used to buy furs,

bribe hunters, win allies, and pacify enemies. In a canoe setting off
for the fur country it made up no less than one-third of the cargo.
"We may truly say that liquor is the root of all evil in the North
West," pronounced Alexander Henry the Younger. And if it was
so, then the traders had only themselves to blame.

So much liquor and bad feeling increased the chances that
violence would be used to solve disputes. Traders assaulted native
and rival alike in their thirst for pelts. Indians filled with lies about
the intentions of this or that stranger were sent to pillage canoes,
burn buildings, even fire on parties of men. The violence reached
a peak during the winter of 1801-02 on the North Saskatchewan.
A young Nor'wester was shot and killed during an argument over
some furs. In an attempt to bring some order to the Northwest the
British Parliament passed the Canada Jurisdiction Act (1803)
giving officials in Lower Canada power to appoint Justices of the
Peace for the Indian territory. But the war continued. "By last
advices the grand crisis was considered as not being far distant,"
reported a determined John Richardson. "We fervently pray that it
may terminate in the ruin and disgrace of our unprincipled
enemy."

As the Canadian rivals battled for supremacy, each recognized
what an advantage it would be to be able to enter the country
through Hudson Bay, now closed to them by the Hudson's Bay
Company charter. Alexander Mackenzie had long harboured
dreams of a united company trading through the Bay. Figuring that
it would be a long time before the Montreal merchants ever
resolved their differences, Mackenzie decided to stage-manage a
takeover of the Hudson's Bay Company. He had Edward Ellice,
the XY agent in London, begin to buy stock on the open market,
and, in 1803, Ellice went so far as to make an outright offer for the
British company — £103,000. But the directors were not interested in bowing out of the Canadian trade and refused to sell.
Meanwhile, Simon McTavish was trying a different approach —
in the summer of 1803 he sent a small army to take the Bay by
force. McTavish's plan was to bully his way right into the heart of
the Hudson's Bay Company empire, establish a small number of
posts, then offer to withdraw them if the Company would give

him a right to export and import cargo through York Fort. The North West Company expedition was armed with musket and cannon but force proved unnecessary. The Hudson's Bay Company men had the good sense not to attack the interlopers but watched from a respectful distance as they threw together a ring of trading houses around the bottom of James Bay. Nor'westers remained in the Bay for three years but the Hudson's Bay Company refused to be impressed. Officials saw McTavish's "invasion" as an elaborate bluff and were not intimidated by the presence of a few scruffy competitors on their territory. Realizing that its bold manoeuvre had failed, the North West Company razed its posts and retreated from the Bay.

The Canadians were rebuffed in Hudson Bay but it really didn't matter. The important competition was taking place in the Northwest where rivalry was taking a heavy toll. Fur returns were falling off; the Indians were becoming hard to deal with, some even withdrawing from the trade; costs were escalating alarmingly. Obviously competition was ruinous, but apparently there was no reconciling the principal rivals. "I see no means of bringing about a coalition for several years to come," wrote Alexander Mackenzie, "by which time the Trade may be reduced if not ruined. . . ."

However, an opportunity suddenly presented itself. On July 6, 1804, Simon McTavish died, leaving his young wife, four children, and an unfinished stone mansion. His body was laid to rest behind the house which stood for another half century gathering moss and creepers and a reputation for being haunted until it was finally pulled down. With "The Marquis" gone, the way was clear for the two old drinking companions, Mackenzie and McGillivray, to make up their differences. Before the year ended the details of a merger had been worked out. The XY Company joined the North West Company and the Canadian trade was once again united and stronger than ever.

The new, united company faced its future without Alexander Mackenzie at its council tables. Only forty years old, he nevertheless had had enough of the fur business and anyway, the years of competition must have left many bruised feelings and betrayed loyalties. "With him and McGillivray there will, I fear, never be intimacy," observed one Montreal merchant. Mackenzie was a celebrity in Canada and England as well. His book about his explorations had won him acclaim and a knighthood; he was recognized wherever he went. In 1804 he won election to the legislative assembly in Lower Canada but it turned out that political life did not suit him. "I am heartily tired of Legislation," he wrote to his nephew. "I sincerely wish that those who thought themselves my friends in being the means of getting me to so honourable a situation had been otherwise employed." He left Canada in 1805 for England and returned to the country of his greatest accomplishments only for short visits.

CHAPTER FIVE

Race Across the Rockies

On May 23, 1797, a young trader named David Thompson walked away from an isolated Hudson's Bay Company post in northern Manitoba and into the service of the North West Company. In the combative world of the fur trade, defection was a common enough event, but David Thompson was more than just another mutinous servant with a grudge against the Company. A skilled surveyor, an experienced inland traveller, an officer in the Company's chain of command, he was, at twenty-seven, already a veteran of thirteen years in the fur country. His great work was still ahead of him, but even so his knowledge of the interior and the opposition made him a prize catch for the Nor'westers.

Thompson was born in London to Welsh parents. His father died when he was baby, and he was raised in poverty by his mother. He attended the charitable Grey Coat School where he prepared for a career with the Royal Navy, but in 1783 peace came, the navy cut back on recruitment and the next year he joined the Hudson's Bay Company instead as an apprentice to the fur trade on the distant shores of North America. Thompson spent his first year in the Bay under the command of Samuel Hearne at Prince of Wales Fort; then a year at York Factory before going inland for a five-year stint on the Saskatchewan. He was an earnest young man, a teetotaller who used to load kegs of brandy on the wildest pack animals hoping they would be dashed to pieces before they reached the Indians. He was pious to the point of superstition. One summer he took to playing draughts to while away his spare time. In his memoirs he records straightfacedly a game he had with Satan who appeared one evening and challenged him. Thompson bested the Devil, but nonetheless took the visitation very seriously, swearing off games of chance forever.

In December 1788, while serving inland, Thompson tumbled down the steep bank of the Saskatchewan and fractured his leg, an accident which in his own words "turned out to be the best thing that ever happened to me." Complications developed and for more than a year he convalesced at Cumberland House. Luckily for Thompson, the accomplished surveyor Philip Turnor was also at Cumberland House during this time and the young invalid took advantage of the idle months to get an education. He brushed up on his mathematics, learned astronomy, and mastered the use of the telescope, the chronometer, and all the other machinery of the surveyor's art. It was the beginning of Thompson's career as surveyor and mapmaker. When he recovered he was set to work looking for a new route from Hudson Bay to the Athasbasca country. The usual passage up Churchill River and across the Methye Portage was fine for Nor'westers coming from Canada, but the Hudson's Bay Company hoped to find a more northerly supply route. As it turned out, the northern route was a chimera; the rivers were not deep enough and were blocked by ice for too long each spring. But Thompson applied himself to the search with vigour, convinced that a back door to Athabasca led through Reindeer Lake and the rivers beyond. He was engaged in following up this theory when he quit the Hudson's Bay Company and joined the opposition.

Why did he defect? Thompson himself said he left the Honourable Company because he was not being given freedom to pursue his surveying work. And this is true, as far as it goes. Just prior to his departure the young servant was made "Master to the Northward" with responsibility for the fur trade, not exploration. The Company was chronically short-staffed in this period and could not afford to have men spending time on projects that did not bear fruit immediately. Skeptics have argued that Thompson also bolted because he feared the responsibilities of leadership for which the Company seemed to have marked him. Whatever his motives, and they were probably mixed, his decision turned out to be a wise one. The North West Company was wealthier and had more men to spare than its opponent. What's more, it had a special interest in finding new, speedier routes to the interior. As the fur trade expanded to the foot of the Rocky Mountains and down the Mackenzie River toward the Arctic, the cost of transportation was becoming extremely burdensome. The situation was not as critical for the British company which enjoyed access through Hudson Bay, but the Canadians despaired at seeing so much of their profits being eaten up getting men and supplies to the fur country. One solution was to break the stranglehold on the Bay route, either by force or by negotiation, and the Nor'westers tried both. Another solution was to seek a completely new route to the western fur country. Since before La Vérendrye, explorers from Canada had sought the elusive "westward flowing river" that would carry them across the continent to the "Western Sea." Peter Pond had hoped to find this river far to the north. His protegé Alexander Mackenzie corrected Pond's geography and actually reached the Pacific Ocean by travelling overland from the Athabasca. But to make the dream a reality, a navigable water passage was needed connecting the ocean to the interior and neither Pond nor Mackenzie nor anyone else had as yet found it. This was the great enterprise David Thompson was destined to complete.

After joining the North West Company, Thompson was sent to probe the passes of the Rocky Mountains in search of a way across them into British Columbia. While he was occupied at this task, another Nor'wester was approaching the Pacific by an entirely different route. A native of Vermont, Simon Fraser came to Upper Canada as part of the Loyalist migration following the American War of Independence. His father died in a rebel prison and young Simon settled with his mother near Cornwall. He was sent to school in Montreal, the fur trade capital, and, through the intercession of relatives, in 1792 he became an apprentice clerk with the North West Company; nine years later he was a partner. Competition with the XY Company checked the expansion of the fur trade for a few years, but in 1805, after the two companies united, Fraser was sent up the Peace River, following in Alexander Mackenzie's footsteps to investigate the virgin hunting grounds of northern British Columbia, what came to be called New Caledonia. Fraser's intention was to locate the river Mackenzie had called the Columbia and follow it to its mouth, hoping that it would prove to be a navigable trade route to the Pacific. He established several posts in the new territory, the first settlements west of the Rockies in British Columbia, and after waiting for the necessary men and supplies to arrive, embarked on the river in May 1808.

As it turned out, the expedition was not following the Columbia after all, but a river later explorers would call the Fraser. After leaving Fort George (the modern Prince George), Fraser and his men had a few days of easy paddling, but soon they confronted their first stretch of violent water and the real horror of the river was exposed to them. The banks had closed around the expedition until they were too steep for portaging, so the men had no choice but to hurl themselves down the foaming cataract in their canoes. One of the craft was sent with five of the best *voyageurs* to discover the safest passage, but the rushing water swept it against a large boulder part way through the rapid, the men just managing to save themselves by clambering atop the rock. Fraser and the rest made their way on foot down the precipitous banks to reach the marooned men. Cutting steps into the slope with their knives, they managed to haul the loaded canoe out of the water and up the cliffside. "In this manner our situation was extremely precarious;" wrote Fraser; "our lives hung as it were upon a thread; for failure of the line or a false step of one of the men might have hurled the whole of us into eternity." Finally admitting that the river at this spot was unnavigable, Fraser ordered the canoes and supplies carried across the mountainous terrain to the bottom of the rapid where the expedition re-embarked. Local Indians told him he was crazy, that the river could not be passed, that he should strike out overland. "But going to the sea by an indirect way was not the object of the undertaking," Fraser observed. "I therefore would not deviate and continued our route according to my original intention."

The river continued to be broken by long stretches of white water littered with rocks and menacing whirlpools. Yet the sides of the canyons were too abrupt to allow for portaging. Instead Fraser lightened the canoes, ran them through the rapids, and then sent the crews back along the banks to collect the rest of the cargo. At one point the canyon walls almost touched above their heads as Fraser and his men shot down the rushing ribbon of water. "I scarcely ever saw any thing so dreary, and seldom so dangerous in any country; and at present while I am writing this, whatever way I turn, mountains upon mountains, whose summits are covered with eternal snows, close the gloomy scene."

Finally the river became completely impassable, and Fraser had to leave it for a while, caching the canoes and setting off on foot, each man carrying a pack weighing thirty-five kilograms. At the present site of Lillooet the party returned to the river. Some of the men now proceeded by canoe while the rest kept to narrow Indian trails which wound beside the river. At time they clung to makeshift ladders of poles and vines hanging from the vertical cliff face, swinging in the breeze high above the foaming waters of the river below. "I have been for a long period among the Rocky Mountains," Fraser wrote incredulously, "but have never seen anything equal to this country, for I cannot find words to describe our situation at times. We had to pass where no human being should venture." By now Fraser realized that he was not travelling the Columbia, that instead he was on another river, one which was too wild to be of any use to the fur trade. Nevertheless, he kept on, and thirty-six days after starting out he arrived at the Indian village of Musqueam at the river's mouth. The local people were unfriendly so the explorer did not linger. He hurried back up the river, and arrived at Fort George on August 6.

Simon Fraser has never enjoyed the fame of Alexander Mackenzie or David Thompson. He was one of the many explorer-traders who eliminated impractical trade routes rather than discovering useful ones. His voyage to the Pacific was an epic of courage, skill, and endurance, but it was also futile. The river was impassable. Fraser left New Caledonia and the North West Company looked elsewhere for its passage to the Pacific.

While Simon Fraser was carrying the fur trade into New Caledonia, David Thompson was at Rocky Mountain House at the headwaters of the Saskatchewan continuing his search for a more southerly route through the Rockies. A major roadblock to this project was the enmity of the Indians who did not want intruders disrupting their established patterns of trade. In the previous century the Blackfoot, armed with guns traded from the white men, drove their neighbours, the Kootenay Indians, from the buffalo country into the valleys of the Rocky Mountains. Then the Blackfoot, or more specifically, the Piegans, part of the Blackfoot nation, threw up a blockade, guarding the headwaters and canyon walls so that traders could not reach their old enemies and supply them with guns. For many years the blockade was successful, until 1807 when the Piegans were drawn south toward the Missouri country on an errand of revenge and David Thompson was able to venture across the mountains unmolested. Thompson did contact the Kootenays and just as the Piegans feared, he began to supply them with arms. In the next few years hostilities increased between the two groups and the Kootenays were able to battle their way back onto the plains to hunt buffalo. The Piegans naturally resented the traders and made life difficult for Thompson on future expeditions. But in 1807 the more immediate result of his trip across the mountains was his arrival at the banks of the Columbia River.

The Columbia flows north out of Windermere Lake for many kilometres parallel with the Rocky Mountains before doubling back on itself in a great arc and flowing south through southeastern British Columbia and central Washington state to the Pacific. When Thompson reached it, he inferred from its northward flow that it would not lead him where he wanted to go and instead of heading downstream he made his way upriver to Windermere Lake where he built Kootenae House and passed the winter. In the next couple of years Thompson continued to be deceived by the river, which he called the Kootenae, not realizing it was the avenue to the Pacific he sought. He travelled widely below the forty-ninth parallel in what is now northern Idaho and Montana, establishing trading posts and winning the Indians to the North West Company. He was not getting any closer to the western ocean but he was gathering a rich harvest of furs and he was laying claim to a vast territory beyond the Rockies where the North West Company hoped to be granted a trade monopoly by the British government. Then, in 1810, Thompson's leisurely pace was disrupted. When he arrived that year at Rainy Lake on his way to the rendezvous at Fort William he was met with urgent orders to return immediately across the Rockies and proceed at last to the Pacific. The Americans had launched a bold challenge to North West Company claims to the Columbia territory and Thompson was needed there to oppose them.

For many years the fur business in American territory had been dominated by Canadian manpower and Canadian capital. With little respect for boundaries, *voyageurs* and *bourgeois* from Montreal travelled wherever the rivers led and Indians were hungry for trade goods. While the "pedlars from Quebec" were making their way to the banks of the Saskatchewan and into the Athabasca country, their comrades at Detroit and Michilimackinac fanned out south and west of the Great Lakes, reaching as far as the waters of the upper Mississippi. Furs from this "southern trade" at times accounted for half the pelts exported from Montreal. When Canadian pre-eminence south of the lakes was finally challenged at the end of the eighteenth century it was less a result of American initiative than of British indifference. The first hint of a change in the status quo was the Treaty of Paris, the agreement which ended the American War of Independence in 1783. Under the terms of the treaty, Great Britain surrendered the huge fur territory south of the Great Lakes to the United States and agreed to hand over its military outposts in the area. Petitioned by Canadian financial interests, the British government dragged its feet about honouring its commitment, offering several pretexts why its soldiers should remain in position, and traders from north of the border continued to do business as usual. But after several years of negotiation the British in 1796 agreed to relinquish the border posts and hand over the "Old Northwest." Canadians were permitted to trade in American territory as long as they obtained a license and paid the appropriate import duties on their goods, but a series of niggling regulations made it quite clear that traders from Montreal would soon be unwelcome across the border. As a result some merchants shifted their attention to the Canadian West, among them the men who combined to form the XY Company. However, others put up with the new situation and continued to send expeditions below the border.

Farther to the west, out on the plains, Canadian traders also dominated the trade of the Missouri River, launching expeditions from their posts on the Red and Assiniboine rivers. As long as Spain owned the western interior these interlopers from the north were unchallenged, but in 1803 the United States purchased the Louisiana territory and things began to change in the Far West as well. First of all, President Thomas Jefferson sent an expedition under Merriweather Lewis and William Clark to explore the territory, to locate a water passage across it to the Pacific, to study the various Indian nations and to collect information about soil and climate that might be useful to future settlers. Lewis and Clark travelled up the Missouri River, crossed the Rocky Mountains and reached the Pacific via the lower Columbia River early in November 1805. After wintering at the mouth of the river they returned overland to St. Louis full of stories about the rich fur resources of the "new Northwest." It didn't take long for merchants in St. Louis to get organized and begin establishing trading posts on the upper Missouri all the way to the Rockies. Here, as elsewhere, Canadians began to retreat from territory they had been used to calling their own.

There was one region, however, distant from the seats of authority, which was so little known that it was an open question who had jurisdiction over it. This was the Columbia, where American laws did not apply and what mattered most was who got there first with enough strength to monopolize the trade. While

David Thompson had been gradually establishing the North West Company's presence in the Columbia district, in New York the American fur merchant John Jacob Astor was plotting his own Pacific adventure. Astor's company was the American Fur Company. One day it would be the dominant force in the American trade but for the time being Astor's strength was centred in the "Old Northwest" between the Mississippi and the Great Lakes. He was opposed there by the Michilimackinac Company, a subsidiary of the North West Company trading out of Montreal. The success of the Canadian concern depended on a free flow of goods and men across the border with the United States. This was by no means a certainty as the mind of Congress was very changeable and from season to season the Nor'westers might find the border closed to their brigades. In such an unstable situation, partners were receptive when Astor approached them with the makings of a deal. An American partner, they calculated, would allow them to get around any restrictions which might be imposed on the trade from Canada. Astor at first wanted to be let in on the company's trade west of the Rockies, but when this proposal was rebuffed he returned with an offer to buy half of the Michilimackinac Company if the Nor'westers would take a one-third interest in the Pacific venture he was planning. Despite some squabbling, the Canadians agreed. After all, Astor seemed to be going ahead anyway so why not get a piece of the action? But before the partnership was finalized the Canadians learned their trans-border trade would be safe from legislative interference for at least another season. Seeing no profit in allying themselves with Astor, they backed out of the deal and left him to mount the Columbia expedition on his own. And for good measure they ordered David Thompson that summer of 1810 back across the Rockies to carry the North West Company standard to the mouth of the Columbia.

Thompson travelled the familiar Saskatchewan River route across the continent, intending to follow its headwaters into the Rockies. In October, as he approached the mountains, he and his Indian guides went ahead of the canoes on horseback to hunt for food, agreeing to meet at a pre-arranged rendezvous. When the canoes did not appear Thompson sent a small party to look for them. He worried about meeting unfriendly Indians and he warned the search party to go carefully and not to fire their guns. Just as he feared, his men returned with news that a group of Piegans were apparently blocking the river, and, to make matters worse, Thompson's men had fired a gun to warn the canoes. Cursing their stupidity in alerting the Indians, Thompson decided to "run for our lives" into the mountains instead of making further attempts to reach his canoes. Historians have debated this curious episode in Thompson's career but there seems little doubt that he ran away and hid. He himself skips briefly over the period in his published *Narrative*, and his journals for the days in question have disappeared. The fact remains that Thompson fled from the Indians, went into hiding in a heavy wood atop a high cliff, and left it to someone else to get his expedition safely underway again.

On October 5 the veteran Nor'wester Alexander Henry arrived at Rocky Mountain House on the upper Saskatchewan and found Thompson's missing canoes waiting there. At that moment the surveyor was downriver, hiding from the Piegans, but Henry did not know that. He assumed that Thompson was up the river waiting for the rest of his expedition to join him, so Henry set himself the task of somehow sneaking the brigade past the suspicious Indians. The Piegans were indeed determined to keep the traders from penetrating the mountains with more arms and ammunition for their enemies. They kept a close watch on the river and loitered belligerently around the trading post. On one occasion Henry dispatched the canoes under the cover of darkness, but the Indians stopped them and ordered them back to the post. Finally he tried an elaborate subterfuge. Unloaded canoes were sent off innocently downriver, apparently to collect some cargo which Henry had cached earlier. When darkness fell the brigade turned back, and, while Henry plied the Indians with enough liquor and laudanum to leave them senseless, the canoes slipped quietly past the post. Just as Henry watched the last of them disappear safely around the point, another party of Indians appeared at the fort, and he had to sedate them in the same way before he could send cargo out to the waiting brigade. Very early the next morning the post-master himself sneaked up the river and erased any marks in the dirt that would give away the deception.

Henry was risking much to outsmart the Indians. If they discovered what he had done, they might exact a high price. So his exasperation must have been total when no sooner had the loaded canoes embarked than one of David Thompson's men arrived with the news that the explorer was camped downriver, not above as Henry had supposed. Henry set out to meet him and found him "starving and waiting for his people" and determined to abandon the Saskatchewan River for a safer route farther to the north. Once again the canoes had to be spirited past Rocky Mountain House under cover of darkness, this time in the opposite direction, and once again the Indians had to be distracted so they would not know they had been deceived. "I was happy to get clear of those canoes," Henry wrote in his journal, "that had caused me so much trouble and anxiety ever since my arrival."

Reunited with the rest of his expedition, Thompson swung north, planning to cross the mountains via the headwaters of the Athabasca River. Early in December he arrived at what would be the jumping-off point for his climb through the mountains and settled into camp to make snowshoes and sleds and prepare for the arduous trip ahead. Once underway, the expedition advanced by heading as far as it could up one of the many small brooks which trailed out of the mountains, then hauling supplies across a height of land in search of another stream bed leading deeper in among the towering peaks. Temperatures dipped well below freezing, the snow deepened, and game animals were scarce. Progress slowed to six kilometres a day. Singly and in groups Thompson's men deserted him and fled back to Rocky Mountain House. But the remnant of the expedition pressed steadily forward, and mid-January found it camped on a mountainside beneath a sparkling glacier at the eighteen-hundred-metre level with only the downhill trek ahead.

At the end of January 1811, Thompson and his men reached the banks of the river he called the Kootenae and settled in to wait the change of seasons. The explorer planned to manufacture bark canoes to carry the expedition to the Pacific but in March he discovered the local birch trees could not provide the necessary materials. Instead he made a single canoe, twenty-five feet long, by sewing together six-inch cedar boards with pine roots.

In April, Thompson and three *voyageurs* set off. If they had followed the flow of the river northward they would have found that it curved south towards the ocean but Thompson feared the unknown Indians who lived in that direction. Upriver he was in familiar territory where the Indians were trading partners and where he could find more men to join his expedition as guides and hunters. Fighting the current and the spring ice the four men worked their way to the head of the Columbia (for that's what Thompson's "Kootenae" actually was), crossed to the actual Kootenay River and descended into northern Montana. Swinging westward, they passed via the trading posts Thompson had established on earlier expeditions to the thunderous Kettle Falls on the lower Columbia. His goal now within reach, Thompson proceeded eagerly down the river and on July 14, 1811, arrived at the Pacific Ocean to find that the Americans were already there.

John Jacob Astor had sent off two expeditions to the Columbia the previous year, one by sea and the other overland. The three-hundred-ton sailing ship *Tonquin* was the first to arrive. It brought a party of about thirty *voyageurs*, clerks, and partners, most of them Canadians and former Nor'westers recruited by Astor in Montreal. The *Tonquin* dropped anchor at the river's mouth in March 1811. Members of the expedition quickly threw up a tiny cluster of log huts and called it Astoria. This was the settlement where Thompson arrived later in the year. The establishment of Astoria appeared to be a triumph for American initiative, but the settlement was not allowed to sink its roots very deep. In 1813 a party of Nor'westers arrived with the news that war had broken out between the United States and Great Britain. The British were sending a warship to capture Astoria, the Nor'westers warned, so why didn't the Americans just surrender now and save everyone a lot of trouble? Fearing a possible bombardment and the destruction of the post, the Astorians decided to strike a deal, and in October they sold the post to the North

West Company for $58,000. The following month a British ship actually did arrive to take formal possession of the area. Canadian fur traders now had a free hand in the vast territory west of the Rockies and north of the Columbia. At least there was one place below the forty-ninth parallel where Canadians were not being forced out of the trade.

When David Thompson found that he had been beaten to the mouth of the Columbia he turned around and headed back upriver, hoping to convince the Indians to take their furs to the interior Canadian posts rather than to the Americans. Following the Columbia past the Kettle Falls, he travelled northwards against the current across the Arrow Lakes and around the great bend in the river where he spied on the riverbank the low hut in which he and his men had waited out the winter earlier in the year. For the first time Thompson realized that his Kootenae was the Columbia; he had found the "westward flowing river" to the Pacific, the last link in the highway of navigable waterways stretching across the entire continent. In the years that followed, the route he pioneered across the Rockies through Athabasca Pass became the gateway to New Caledonia, the most travelled pathway from the prairies to the Pacific slope. Similarly, the lower Columbia became the southern leg of a far-flung transportation system that connected the interior posts of New Caledonia by pack animal and canoe with the Pacific.

David Thompson left the West in 1812. He was forty-two years old and had spent twenty-eight years enduring the hardships and uncertainties of life and trade in the "Indian territory." With his mixed-blood wife Charlotte and a growing brood of children, he retired to Terrebonne where he set to work making maps of the country he knew so intimately. First of all he produced a map of the West for the North West Company, a copy of which hung in the great hall at Fort William. A second, more detailed map of the West was purchased by the government of Upper Canada, and for the next fifty years it was the source for all the maps done of the area. Thompson continued this work for several years, and it was not until 1843 that the British government received from him the final maps based on the extensive detail of his many surveys. But long before his map-making was done, Thompson had to find gainful employment. Unlike many of his predecessors who retired from the fur country to stone mansions and a life of ease, Thompson was not a wealthy man, and he had a large family to support. In 1815 the Thompsons moved to a farm in Glengarry, and for ten years he worked again as a surveyor, plotting the Ontario section of the boundary between the United States and Canada. He then made an unsuccessful attempt at business, and getting himself into a critical financial position, he returned to surveying, the one thing he knew well. In his late sixties he was still out in the bush doing survey work around the Muskoka Lakes, in the Eastern Townships, and along the St. Lawrence. Finally, the man who had mapped the West, crossed the Rockies on foot countless times, found the Columbia River and followed it to the Pacific, was reduced to surveying city streets for a living.

Thompson's memoirs, his great *Narrative*, now considered a classic work of Canadian literature, was conceived late in his life as a scheme to make money. The idea was that a group of subscribers would form a company and pay him a salary of $30 a month while he wrote the book. In return his patrons would take half of the profits earned by the published work. But the book was never finished. Thompson spent six years writing and rewriting while his health failed and his eyesight dimmed. The arrangement did not solve his financial problems and towards the end he had to sell his surveying equipment and even some of his clothes to make ends meet. He was still working sporadically at the book at his death in 1857 but it was not complete and for several years the manuscript disappeared. Eventually it came into the hands of J. B. Tyrrell, the eminent geologist and historian, who published it for the first time in 1916, more than half a century after its author's death.

Alexander Mackenzie. *A veteran of pioneering expeditions to the Arctic and Pacific oceans, Mackenzie was a driving force behind the XY Company in its rivalry with the North West Company. Public Archives of Canada (C-1348)*

The rendezvous. American trappers who worked the beaver meadows of the Rocky Mountains met each summer with their suppliers from the East at a grand rendezvous. Indian groups also came to the rendezvous to trade and feast. *Public Archives of Canada (C-439)*

Simon McTavish
"*The Marquis*" *of the
Montreal trade,
McTavish is credited with
moulding the independent
Canadian traders into a
strong, united company,
the North West
Company. Public
Archives of Canada
(C-164)*

William McGillivray.
*After taking over the
leadership of the North
West Company when his
uncle, McTavish, died,
McGillivray commanded
it through the years of the
great competition with the
Hudson's Bay Company.
This painting was done
just a year before the two
fierce rivals merged in
1821. Public Archives of
Canada (C-167)*

York boats depart York Factory, 1821. *York Factory was the Hudson's Bay Company's trans-shipment centre. Furs were brought here from all across the fur country and loaded onto ships from England which had just unloaded their cargoes of supplies and trade goods. By the time this painting was made, the York boat had replaced the canoe as the main carrier on the Company's transportation network. Public Archives of Canada (C-1918)*

The portage. *York boats carried more cargo than canoes but they were much heavier to portage. Unlike a bark canoe, which could be carried on the shoulders of a single* voyageur, *the planked York boat was hauled across a "road" of logs. At longer portages oxen were sometimes used. Public Archives of Canada (C-1922)*

The trading ceremony. *Speechifying was an important part of the trading ceremony. The native leader customarily described events which had taken place since he was last at the post, made complaints about the quality of trade goods and asked for fair treatment. This painting was made at Red River in 1825. The chief is addressing the governor of the colony through an interpreter. His men are engaged in that other important trading ritual, smoking. Public Archives of Canada (C-1939)*

Chief factor on the move. *Fur trade officials moved around the territory with a fair amount of ceremony. This painting shows the governor of Red River, in his beaver top hat, being transported by a crew of* voyageurs. *Public Archives of Canada (C-1944)*

Buffalo hunting camp. *This painting by William Armstrong shows buffalo meat drying in the prairie sun. After they dried the strips of meat were pounded and made into pemmican which was delivered in skin bags to trading posts across the fur country. Public Archives of Canada (C-10502)*

Voyageurs at dawn. *Frances Hopkins captured this* voyageurs' *camp just as canoemen were rousing themselves in the morning. Public Archives of Canada (C-2773)*

Colin Robertson.
Robertson, a former Nor'wester, led the Hudson's Bay Company's penetration of the Athabasca country in the years before 1821. Public Archives of Canada (C-8984)

The voyageur. *These Canadian canoemen were sketched in the 1820s. Public Archives of Canada (C-9461)*

Red River farm. *This painting by William G. R. Hind shows a typical home in the Red River settlement. The Red River cart was the primary means of land transport in the fur country. A cart was made entirely of wood, including the axle, and in the words of one historian, it "shrieked like a lost soul" as it rolled across the plains. Public Archives of Canada (C-13965)*

Prairie Indian camp. *William Armstrong made this painting in 1867 when there were still buffalo to hunt on the plains. Public Archives of Canada (C-10500)*

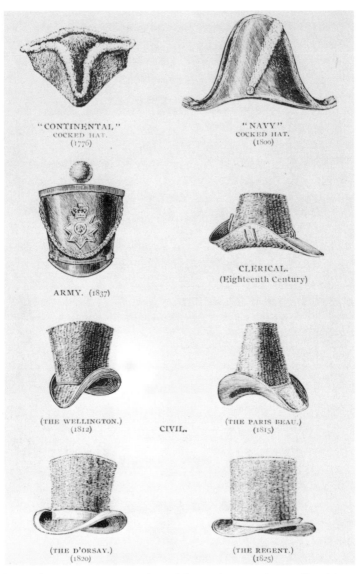

"CONTINENTAL"
COCKED HAT.
(1776)

"NAVY"
COCKED HAT.
(1800)

ARMY. (1837)

CLERICAL.
(Eighteenth Century)

(THE WELLINGTON.)
(1812)

CIVIL.

(THE PARIS BEAU.)
(1815)

(THE D'ORSAY.)
(1820)

(THE REGENT.)
(1825)

Beaver hats. *Beaver was popular with hatters because of its excellent felting qualities. These are some of the styles favoured in the European* beau monde. *Public Archives of Canada (C-17338)*

York Factory, 1853. *The headquarters of the Hudson's Bay Company in the Northwest, York Factory began as a simple log post in 1683. Notice the board sidewalks to keep pedestrians above the mud. Public Archives of Canada (C-16826)*

The long haul. *At the portage* voyageurs *carried goods in packages weighing about forty kilograms each. Public Archives of Canada (C-19041)*

Fort Vancouver.
For many years the headquarters of the Hudson's Bay Company on the Columbia River, Fort Vancouver was succeeded as the western depot by Fort Victoria in 1849. Public Archives of Canada (C-19121)

Peter Skene Ogden.
Ogden's career in the West lasted from 1810, when he joined the North West Company, to his death in 1854. Public Archives of Canada (C-27147)

George Simpson. *The "Little Emperor" was "ruler in residence" of western Canada from 1821 to his death in 1860. Public Archives of Canada (C-23580)*

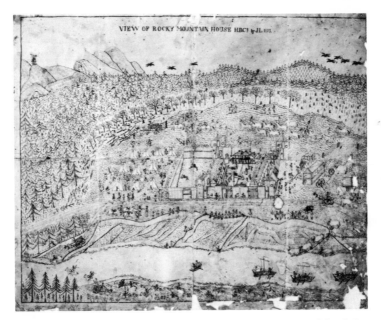

Rocky Mountain House, 1873. *This drawing shows many of the daily activities at a fur trade post in the nineteenth century. To the left of the post is the Indian "plantation." Above it, logs are being collected for a construction project. Within the palisades, on the left, two men are tending the vegetable garden. Three York boats are setting off downriver. Public Archives of Canada/National Map Collection (C-16082)*

CHAPTER SIX

The Battle for Athabasca

The North West Company emerged from its struggle with the XY Company ready to dominate the fur trade in the West. Led by William McGillivray, nephew of "The Marquis" Simon McTavish, the Nor'westers were at last free of obstruction from other Montreal merchants, free to concentrate on their remaining rival, the "Honourable Company" on the shores of Hudson Bay. During the competition with the XYs, Canadian traders had indulged their love of bluster and intimidation to the limit. By 1805 violence and extortion were as much a part of their strategy as bargaining and gift-giving. But the Nor'westers had also developed a skill at outflanking their opponents and shown a remarkable zeal for exploration and discovery. Already Alexander Mackenzie had reached the western ocean; within a few years another Nor'wester, David Thompson, would penetrate the Rockies and journey the length of the Columbia. Against such a combination of enthusiasm and force the Hudson's Bay Company was momentarily on the ropes. So much were the Nor'westers apparently in command that it was claimed they actually wanted the British company to remain in business as a "Cloak to protect the trade from more active opponents." However, as the first decade of the century drew to a close the Hudson's Bay Company began to gain in strength and determination, and the final contest for control of the fur trade began in earnest. No less was at stake than the spoils of half a continent. It was a vicious rivalry, wasteful and violent and reflecting credit on no one. Each side liked to point with injured innocence to the atrocities of the other, but both were defending the only principle that mattered to them, the right to harvest the fur resources of the West unhindered by competitors or governments. Eventually the contest exhausted the rivals and they fell into each other's arms like two punch drunk boxers.

The Hudson's Bay Company in the first decade of the nineteenth century was on the defensive. Against the determination of the Canadians, it could muster only token opposition. In Athabasca, the treasure house of the trade, the Company could not even maintain a single post. When Peter Fidler tried to get established there, the Nor'westers kept the Indians away and terrorized his men by prowling around the house shooting off their guns and howling like wolves until finally the post was abandoned. The Nor'westers were simply toying with the Company, reported its chief trader at York, "that while we nibble at a sprat they may catch whales unmolested in the north." Hudson's Bay Company servants saw themselves as traders, not brawlers. They were unwilling to meet their rivals blow for blow and, as a result, were treated like "old women who had not courage even to defend the furs which they had obtained." The inland posts were dilapidated, "infinitely below what an Ourang-Outang would have contented himself with," and the servants went about the countryside so timidly that they dared not even carry their mail freely between posts, preferring to sew it inside their coats or cache it in a frozen fish.

The Napoleonic Wars then raging in Europe were responsible for much of the Company's difficulty. Whenever Britain was engaged in an international conflict the Company had trouble finding capable servants in sufficient numbers. Now that the trade had spread all the way across the West the need for these servants was even greater than usual. What's more, war disrupted the European market for furs, cutting into sales at a time when the demand for many types of pelts was in decline anyway. The

Company had less capital to reinvest in the trade at a time when it needed more manpower and extra resources to meet the challenge of a strong competitor.

Faced with this tangle of difficulties, Company directors prepared to abandon the fur trade altogether. Given that a dozen years later the Hudson's Bay Company gained complete control of the West, it is astonishing how close it came in 1810 to withdrawing from the fur business. The reason it did not do so was that the essentially rudderless group of directors was suddenly brought to life by a trio of kinsmen with new ideas about the trade and a plan to use the Company as a vehicle for their own interests in the West. These men — Thomas Douglas, Lord Selkirk; his wife's brother, Andrew Wedderburn Colville; and his wife's cousin, John Halkett — began to buy stock in the Company in 1806. Surprisingly, it was not very difficult to buy an influential voice in the leadership of the Hudson's Bay Company. Alexander Mackenzie estimated that £20,000 would bring control of the Company since there was only a little over £100,000 of stock issued, meetings of the directors were poorly attended, and proxies were seldom used. In fact, Mackenzie was involved in just such a manoeuvre on behalf of the North West Company. Had he been successful he would have brought the two companies together and the Northwest would have been spared a decade of tragedy and violence. But unfortunately for him, Mackenzie allied himself with Lord Selkirk, a man whose aims were secretly quite opposed to those of the Nor'westers. Before Mackenzie realized what was happening, Selkirk and his relations had enough stock to be a deciding voice in the inner sanctum of the Company and the North West Company was shut out. The last chance that the fur trade rivalry might be settled peacefully in a London boardroom, rather than forcibly in the western woods, was lost.

The Selkirk faction had decided opinions about the fur trade. These were drawn up by Colville, adopted by the company, and implemented as the "Retrenching System." In essence, the purpose of the new system was to stiffen the backbone of servants in the field, give them some cause to extend themselves on the Company's behalf, and apply some economy to wasteful branches of the trade. Any attempt to get established in Athabasca was put on the back burner, traders were given a share of the profits, accounting procedures were streamlined, and an attempt was made to hire more enterprising servants. Most importantly, the Company agreed to become a party to the colonizing zeal of Lord Selkirk and granted him more than three hundred thousand square kilometres of territory on the banks of the Red River to establish an agricultural settlement. From this colony the Company hoped to obtain a steady supply of servants and foodstuffs. Directors could not have anticipated the harvest of intrigue and heartbreak which would also be reaped from Lork Selkirk's adventure.

Red River was not the first attempt by Selkirk to establish an agricultural colony for dispossessed Scottish highlanders.

Selkirk had been born in 1771, the last of seven sons, and as a young man there was no reason to think he would be anything but a gentleman farmer content with a small share of the family wealth. However, one by one his elder brothers died, and, in 1799, plain Thomas Douglas became the Fifth Earl of Selkirk. Selkirk was a peer with a social conscience. Living in London, moving in wealthy aristocratic circles, he was involved in public affairs and took a special interest in the question of emigration. His first colony was on Prince Edward Island where he settled eight hundred Scottish immigrants in 1803. A second, much less successful venture was at Baldoon in Upper Canada. Since first reading about the Red River country Selkirk had believed it was ideally suited for one of his colonies, but the Hudson's Bay Company charter seemed to stand in the way of any further action. Selkirk went ahead with his other settlements, but he began to buy stock in the Company with an eye to one day making it part of his designs. In 1809 his purchases became more substantial, and within two years he and his allies had secured a controlling voice on the London Committee.

Technically the Red River colony was Selkirk's project, not the Hudson's Bay Company's. However, the distinction was a fine one which not many observers could make. Selkirk had received his grant of land, five times the size of Scotland, for a token payment of ten shillings. He agreed to provide employees to the Company. His colonists travelled via company posts, were assisted with company supplies, and were, in fact, employed by the Company. No wonder the leaders of the North West Company believed, as Simon McGillivray wrote his brother William, that "the Committee of the Hudson's Bay Co. is at present a mere machine in the hands of Lord Selkirk. . . ." As soon as they got wind of Selkirk's plans the Nor'westers tried to thwart them. In London their agents made a last minute unsuccessful attempt to have the company retract its grant of land. In Scotland Simon McGillivray published anonymous letters in newspapers painting a bleak and terrifying picture of the colony's prospects and warning settlers against signing on. And in the Canadian West the stage was set for a tragic confrontation.

As far as the North West Company was concerned, Selkirk's Red River colony could not be disassociated from the strategy of the fur trade. The colony struck at the heart of the Nor'westers' transportation system. It laid a hostile settlement right across the major rivers connecting the fur country to the plains where the Company's stocks of pemmican were gathered. It also seemed to take for granted that the land was the Hudson's Bay Company's to give away, an assumption which the Canadians did not accept. They argued that Red River was first explored by the French and had passed into Canadian possession at the time of the Conquest. Therefore the colony was illegal as well as impertinent. Lastly, the Nor'westers were convinced that Red River was part of a coordinated plan to establish the British Company in Athabasca, the source of most of their profits. The colony would be producing men and supplies; what else for if not to support an invasion of the northern fur country? Selkirk's settlement could not be allowed to flourish unopposed. "It will require some time," concluded a determined Simon McGillivray, "and I fear much expense to us as well as to himself, before he is driven to abandon the project, and yet he must be driven to abandon it, for his success would strike at the very existence of our Trade."

It seemed at first that bad luck and bad management would combine to abort the enterprise before the Nor'westers had a chance at it. The initial group of about a hundred colonists arrived at York Factory late in September 1811, after a long and dispiriting sail across the Atlantic. The season was too far advanced to consider pushing inland but the colonists could not be accommodated at the post and had to spend the winter squatting in log huts several kilometres up the Nelson River. The dark season did not pass comfortably. Irish and Orkneymen brawled, supplies were inadequate, and an armed mutiny split the camp. It was a thankful group which finally reached Red River in August. Colonists hurried to get their crops planted but the onset of winter forced them to withdraw down the river to the Hudson's Bay Company post at Pembina. Next summer they returned to their land, sowed another crop, and built some cabins before once again sitting out the winter at Pembina. Failure to become self-sufficient posed a problem for the colony's governor, Miles Macdonnell. In lieu of harvested crops he had to rely on local food resources, principally the buffalo, and this brought him into conflict with the North West Company and the local French-speaking, mixed-blood people, the Métis. Assiniboia, as the colony was called, included some of the finest buffalo-hunting territory in the West. Each summer the Métis people went out onto the plains to run the teeming herds. The women butchered the warm carcasses, dried the meat, and made the pemmican which was then carried in bags from the provisioning posts at the edge of the prairie down the Souris, the Qu'Appelle, the Assiniboine, and the Red rivers to the North West Company depot on Lake Winnipeg, where it was distributed to the canoes as they passed on their way to the fur country. Pemmican was the fuel of the fur trade and the livelihood of the Métis. Neither the mixed-bloods nor the Nor'westers could allow the newcomers to interfere with such a vital traffic.

Yet interfere is what Miles Macdonell did in a forthright and dramatic way. In January 1814, the governor issued a proclamation. Worried that his colonists would not have enough food to survive another winter, Macdonell forbade the export of pemmican from Assiniboia without a license granted by him. In the spring he followed up his Pemmican Proclamation by expropriating stocks of pemmican from trading posts in the territory and blockading the river to stop the traditional brigades as they journeyed to Lake Winnipeg. At Fort Douglas, the colony stronghold, guns were mounted overlooking the river and as the boats laden with pemmican converged on the spot it looked as though a violent clash was unavoidable. However, at the last moment a peaceful agreement was negotiated. Macdonell allowed two hundred bags of pemmican to leave the colony in return for a promise that he would receive an equal amount of meat to feed his people the following winter.

The Pemmican War ended peacefully but the seeds of future conflict were sown. The Métis saw that their claim to do as they pleased on land they considered their own was not going to be recognized by the intruders. It did not take much persuasion for the Nor'westers to turn this fear into a grievance and attach the Métis firmly to their cause. The Canadians too were fuming at Macdonell's high-handedness and preparing to stand up to him. "I hope the Ancient North West Spirit will rouse with indignation," wrote William McGillivray to Duncan Cameron in charge of the North West fort in the colony. "Be assured we have as good legal opinion as any in England that we have rights as British subjects which are not to be infringed. In other respects if we suffer our property to be forcibly taken from us it is our own fault." What further encouragement did Cameron need to meet force with force? The North West commander managed to convince quite a few colonists that their prospects in the West were dim and he offered them free passage to Canada in North West canoes. More than forty took him up on his offer and abandoned the place in the spring of 1815. Meanwhile Métis horsemen were harrying the remaining settlers, stealing their livestock and ploughs, shooting off guns, and threatening their crops. Matters came to a head in June when Cameron arrested Miles Macdonnell and packed him off to Fort William, along with 140 colonists. The rest of the settlers tried to hang on but the Métis drove them away by trampling their fields and burning their houses. Early in August nothing remained of Selkirk's colony but three persistent settlers who would not be dislodged, some broken crops, and heaps of smoking ash.

The Nor'westers and the Métis did not have long to celebrate their victory. At the north end of Lake Winnipeg the sixty fugitive colonists hurrying to reach York Factory were overtaken by a Hudson's Bay Company brigade led by Colin Robertson and bound for the fur country. Robertson was a one-time Nor'wester who claimed to have quit the company in revulsion against its bullyboy tactics. He was a determined, imaginative competitor and immediately he rallied the fleeing colonists and led them back to Red River. Under his leadership the colony was re-established, and, late in the fall, a new governor, Robert Semple, arrived with another influx of colonists. Like a phoenix, the tiny settlement rose from the ashes of its defeat.

Naturally enough its opponents were furious and plotted their revenge. The Métis would gather in the spring to march on the settlement, warned their leader Cuthbert Grant, and "it is hoped we shall come off with flying colours and never see any of them again in the Colonizing way in Red River. . . ." Robertson saw the direction in which events were moving and decided to act first. In March he set off with a party of twelve men and captured Fort Gibraltar, the North West post which was generally considered "the Key of the river." With this stronghold in their possession, the colonists could blockade the river and once again stop the pemmican brigades from reaching the North West depot on Lake Winnipeg.

At this point whatever unity held the colony together evaporated. Governor Semple preferred a more cautious strategy than Robertson, and the two men quarrelled over tactics. There was also the leadership of the community at stake, and colonists lined up in two opposing camps behind the men. Seeing that the dispute had turned the colony into "a hotbed of Hypocrisy, desertion and party spirit," Robertson decided to leave, and, on June 11, he departed for York Factory.

Even as Robertson's canoe carried him away from the colony a small army of Métis was approaching from the west. Already this band of warriors had seized the pemmican bound for Fort Douglas and had occupied the Hudson's Bay Company's Brandon House. Not far from the Red River colony they divided into two groups. One would stay where it was while the other, led by Cuthbert Grant, would strike overland, skirting Fort Douglas to blockade the river above the colony and cut off the only avenue of supplies and reinforcements. Apparently the plan was to lay seige to Fort Douglas, not to attack it. On June 19 Grant's party was sighted from the fort, moving across the plain to the northeast. Nor sure what the Métis intended to do, Governor Semple led a few armed men out of the fort to find out. Marching up the road beside the river, they met the Métis beside a clump of trees called Seven Oaks. Neither side seems to have known what to do. Each suspected the other; each was armed and nervous; each drew on years of grievance and prejudice. A Métis emissary advanced to ask Semple what he wanted. Angry words were exchanged, the messenger fled back to his ranks, a shot was fired, and suddenly the tense stillness snapped. The colonists did not stand a chance. They were outnumbered and outflanked and they fell in their tracks or fleeing for cover by the river. Governor Semple took a bullet in the leg and was finished off cold-bloodedly at point-blank range despite Grant's attempts to save him. Twenty-one other colonists died in the skirmish, which lasted a mere fifteen minutes. The next day the victorious Métis accepted the surrender of Fort Douglas. The remaining settlers were dispatched in boats out of the country and the Red River colony once again was eradicated.

Even in the violent history of the fur trade Seven Oaks was an unprecedented stroke. Yet instead of bringing the combatants to their senses, the tragedy only hardened their resolve. Force was now a way of doing business and the law became a blunt instrument of intimidation.

The Canadian Jurisdiction Act had been passed several years before to bring peace to the fur country, but it came to be used arbitrarily by both sides as a weapon of war. Under its provisions traders got themselves appointed magistrates in Canada and arrived in the interior with a sheaf of blank warrants for the arrest of anyone who got in their way. Instead of out-trading an opponent it became common simply to arrest him. Traders were tossed in gaol and hurried off to trial in Canada on the flimsiest pretexts. "Yesterday I was a judge, today I am an Indian trader," boasted one Nor'wester gleefully. The law in the West had become a charade, honoured when it suited one's purposes, otherwise ignored.

The news of Seven Oaks reached Lord Selkirk at Sault Ste. Marie on his way inland. He had arrived the previous year and had spent the winter in Montreal gathering information about the sins of the North West Company and raising his own private army of disbanded soldiers. He was on his way to drive the Nor'westers from Assiniboia when he learned the fate of the colony and he decided to push on to Fort William to get more details.

Selkirk and his contingent arrived at the depot early in August and established their camp about a mile from the fort up the Kaministiquia River. William McGillivray, who was at the post for the annual rendezvous, waited to see what "this pidling Lord" would do. In public at least, McGillivray was not accepting any responsibility for events at Red River. Governor Semple had unaccountably attacked a peaceable band of Métis as they went about their business; there was no blood on the hand of any Nor'wester. Selkirk took a different view. The North West Company had plagued his settlement from the beginning. It had scared off colonists, held back precious food supplies, stirred up the Métis, and now he was convinced its servants were behind the "massacre" at Seven Oaks. In his capacity as a newly-minted magistrate, Selkirk sent nine armed men to arrest the company partners at Fort William. Surprisingly, this audacious assault on the North West Company citadel went off unopposed. McGillivray and the others gave themselves up without a fight and Selkirk moved into the fort. There he found furs stolen from the Hudson's Bay Company and evidence that the Nor'westers had rewarded the Métis for the Seven Oaks affair. Sure now that Fort William "had been used by the North West company as a rendezvous of robbers, and murderers and the receptacle of their plunder," Selkirk and his occupying army sent the prisoners down to Canada for trial and settled in for the winter.

Colin Robertson crowed that Selkirk had "completely laid the axe at the root of the North West influence and jurisdiction in this part of the country," but the Montreal company was not to be dislodged so easily. In fact, events were turning against the colonizing Lord. Later that season the Nor'westers managed to rouse an elderly magistrate near Sault Ste. Marie and rush him to Fort William where he served Selkirk with a warrant. But Selkirk, protected by his little band of mercenaries, refused to acknowledge the magistrate's authority, claiming he was "an old man in his dotage, never by any chance sober after mid-day." The use of warrants had become something of a farce but they were nevertheless legally binding, and Selkirk's peremptory refusal to obey the law seriously discredited him in official circles. In Lower Canada, the Governor, Sir John Sherbrooke, prepared a two-man investigating commission to leave for Fort William as soon as a passage opened in the spring. And in London the Colonial Secretary, Lord Bathurst, exasperated at the "system of violence, which has too long prevailed in the Indian territory," ordered that the rival companies be bound to stop brawling and to restore each other's stolen property. As well, he told Sherbrooke to have the impudent Selkirk arrested and brought to trial, even if it meant sending a troop of soldiers after him. By the time the Nor'westers and the government commission arrived at Fort William in 1817 Selkirk had already left for his colony. While the traders re-occupied their depot the commission pushed on to the settlement. There they conducted inquiries and issued warrants, and by the end of the summer all the principals were returning to Montreal for the last act of the drama. But instead of a quick resolution the legal battle dragged on for years, and no wonder. Selkirk laid 150 charges against the Nor'westers and in return they laid 29 suits against him. The trials were a mockery. Prisoners skipped bail, cases were deferred time and again, and were heard in several different locations. At one point it was decided to start the entire proceedings all over again. Not even Selkirk himself could be bothered to wait around for a final verdict. He returned to London in 1818, his health broken, a dying man.

Even though it was not a trading enterprise, Selkirk's Red River colony influenced the history of the western fur trade dramatically. The tenacity and defiance of the British Lord startled the North West Company, which was used to getting its own way in the fur country. Reputation was an important factor in the Indian trade. The Hudson's Bay Company prided itself on a name for fair dealing and quiet competence. The swaggering Nor'westers, on the other hand, liked to spice their business with an element of fear and intimidation. Events at Red River showed how far the Canadians would go to protect this reputation and defend their interests. The resort to browbeating, even murder, increased the intensity of the rivalry between the companies, fueling resentments and adding to a growing list of grievances. The trade was like a blood feud; each side revenged itself on the other in a never-ending spiral of violence and litigation. Red River exacerbated this contest, but at the same time helped to end it. The British government decided it could no longer countenance so much disruption in its American colonies. Order must be imposed; the colonial office would do it if the principals could not. This resolve was only strengthened by events in Athabasca, the last campaign in the fur trade war.

Ever since Peter Pond had carried the Canadian trade into the Athabasca country the northern lake had been considered the most valuable trading centre in the Northwest. The Nor'westers established themselves like lords, reigning unopposed over the Indians with guile and force. They traded hard, and if the natives did not do as they wanted the Canadians stole their women and held them hostage, brushing all complaints aside. "I told them that we would do as we thought proper," reported one of the North West partners, "for it was not their business to prescribe rules to us. . . ." As a result of such harsh treatment some Indian groups withdrew from the trade. They refused to bring furs and provisions to the posts and even plotted to drive the Canadians out of the country and reclaim it as their own. This was the situation in 1816 when the Hudson's Bay Company launched yet another of its attempts to get a foothold in Athabasca. The company had tried several times before; each time it had been beaten back, either by its own incompetence or by the bullying of its rival. The mastermind behind the last expedition was Colin Robertson, the ex-Nor'wester, who knew how to stand up to his former partners. "When you are among wolves, howl." That was his motto and his strategy.

Robertson had first approached the Hudson's Bay Company with plans for an Athabasca venture in 1810. He could not understand why the Company allowed rivals to trade "at the threshold of your doors" without doing something about it and recommended that a large force of French Canadians, "the best *voyageurs* in the World," be hired in Montreal and dispatched to Athabasca. After putting off the project for several years the London Committee gave Robertson the green light to go to Montreal to organize his expedition.

At first the Athabasca venture seemed doomed to fail like all the others. Robertson did not accompany the canoes, he was sidetracked to Red River where he helped re-establish the faltering colony in the summer of 1815, so the mantle of leadership fell to John Clarke, his lieutenant. Clarke was an impetuous, unreliable man whose own interests usually came well before the Company's. Yet he commanded great loyalty from his men and the Indians seemed to like his flamboyant style. As a second-in-command he was troublesome but productive; as a leader he was a disaster. During the first winter the Hudson's Bay Company men ran low of provisions. Clarke dispersed them throughout the country to fend for themselves. He personally led a party up the Peace River without any food whatsoever, expecting to hunt and trade from the Indians. The North West opposition, practising their "starving system," kept the Indians away until the newcomers were forced to come begging at their door. But even North West provisions, bought at exorbitant prices, could not support all the Hudson's Bay Company servants. Sixteen died before spring returned. The next season Clarke was still in command. This time the Nor'westers wielded their spurious legal powers, arresting several of the competition and even seizing the Hudson's Bay Company post, Fort Wedderburn. After three years the Company was barely able to maintain a fishing camp in Athabasca.

In the summer of 1818 Colin Robertson finally took charge of the expedition he had planned. Passing up the familiar Churchill River route that summer he found his posts "surrounded by the sentinels of our opponents" and his men lucky to find enough food, let alone trade furs. At Fort Wedderburn the Nor'westers from neighbouring Fort Chipewyan "come over every evening in a body calling out our men to pitched battles." Since most of the informants belong to the Hudson's Bay Company, it is not easy to get the North West Company side of the story. The behaviour of its men suggests a company desperate to protect its monopoly at a time when fur returns were falling off, Indians were hostile, and its own men were talking mutiny against the prevailing partnership arrangements. As well, there may have been some truth to the charge that Robertson was trying to incite the local Chipewyans to attack the North West post. In October the Hudson's Bay Company master was jumped outside his own fort by a gang of Nor'westers and spirited off to Fort Chipewyan. The North West leader, John George McTavish, apparently knew nothing of this capture but put the best face he could on it, locking Robertson up to await a Canadian trial the next year.

During the winter the prisoner was allowed to communicate with his men in an open letter which was censored by his captors. To avoid giving away any of his own tactics, and to pass on tidbits of gossip he picked up inside Fort Chipewyan, Robertson devised a system of coded messages. He hid the key to deciphering the code in a keg on its way to Fort Wedderburn. Despite hints in the public letter that the keg needed washing out, the key was not discovered. Trying a different tack, Robertson suddenly developed a taste for Shakespeare and asked his men to send him an edition of the Bard. Inside the book he wrote a message and returned it to his post. A few days later he asked that a quote be checked for him and finally the key was discovered. From then on Robertson and his men kept up a steady correspondence in coded letters smuggled back and forth in kegs of rum until finally, near the end of his imprisonment, their ruse was discovered.

As a result of this communication, the Hudson's Bay Company men, in spite of the absence of their leader, were able to deal a blow to North West hegemony, and Robertson could claim without much exaggeration that "we have gained a complete footing in Athabasca. . . ." In June the prisoner was put aboard a canoe to accompany the annual brigade back to Canada. On the way down he was almost drowned when his canoe, some say not so accidently, was upset in a dangerous rapid, but Robertson survived and at Cumberland House simply walked away from his captors into the Hudson's Bay post.

Meanwhile, news of Robertson's captivity infuriated William Williams, the Hudson's Bay Company chief at York Factory. Williams decided that it was time to "retaliate on these Buccaneers." Equipping himself with the ubiquitous arrest warrants obtained for him in Montreal, Williams gathered a force of Company servants and retired soldiers and set off to waylay the North West brigade as it came down the Saskatchewan from the interior that summer. Dragging a pair of cannon and two swivel guns up the river and across Lake Winnipeg, this small army dug in at the foot of the Grand Rapid, where the Saskatchewan emptied into the lake. As the North West partners walked carelessly down the portage trail, Williams and his followers simply stepped from the underbrush and served their warrants. It was a theatrical coup, carried off with a great deal of bluster but no gunfire. The Nor'westers, who had just lost their own prisoner, Colin Robertson, at Cumberland House, were now the captives. They were carried down to York Factory and dispersed for trial.

Robertson returned to Athabasca for another winter and it was obvious the tide of the battle had turned. Canadians no longer ruled the waterways. They were being out-traded in the field, the Indians were defecting to the Hudson's Bay banner, and, most important, the winterers had lost their enthusiasm for the fight. The next summer Robertson was taken prisoner again, this time at Grand Rapid by a band of Nor'westers mimicking Williams' highjacking of the season before, but really this was an after-thought. In the West the long campaign was over. There was no question now that the two rivals were going to come to some arrangement and soon. It only remained to discover what it would be and that question would be resolved in London, far from the wilderness posts of the North West.

Despite the virulence of competition in the fur country, where traders were willing to starve each other to death or blow each other apart with cannon, the two companies were never really that far from a merger during the two decades of most intense rivalry. Neither the North West Company nor the Hudson's Bay Company was as strong as it liked to pretend. Competition was draining away profits at an alarming rate. Posts proliferated across the West; men had to be hired, transported, and fed. Beaver and other fur animals were slaughtered with no thought for conserva-tion, and native people were tyrannized to the point where they were driven to fight back. There were plenty of good reasons for the rivals to end their struggle. But at the same time the outbreak of peace could not be allowed to jeopardize their basic interests. Surrender was out of the question; what was needed was an agreement which would satisfy the requirements of both com-panies.

At first the answer seemed to be to carve up the Northwest into spheres of influence. In 1811 the Nor'westers suggested that they be given exclusive right of trade in Athabasca and west of the Rocky Mountains, areas which the Hudson's Bay Company had not yet penetrated. In return they would recognize a Hudson's Bay Company monopoly in the Muskrat Country south and west of the Bay and along the South Saskatchewan River. However, the British Company could not accept a proposal which seemed to deny their chartered right to exclusive trade in the lands draining into the Bay. Neither did it want to agree to forego ambitions on the Pacific slope. Four years later Lord Selkirk, who was on his way to Montreal, was empowered by the London Committee to pre-sent the Nor'westers with another partition scheme. But the Canadians had begun to consider the possibility of merger by then. They countered Selkirk's offer with a plan of their own. They proposed joining the two companies into a single operation. One-third of the capital for this concern would be put up by the Hudson's Bay Company and two-thirds by the North West Company, with profits shared in the same proportions. If this scheme had been adopted, perhaps twenty-three lives would have been spared at Seven Oaks. But it was not. Negotiators did not agree how management of the new company would be shared and talks broke off. Selkirk led his army to the interior and competition ran its wasteful course.

Since partition and merger had both failed for the time being, the North West Company decided to have another try at buying out its opponent. Selkirk, who owned a controlling share of the stock, was the sticking point. The Lord was ill and growing tired of the endless troubles his Red River colony brought him. Still he was determined that the settlement must survive. He was afraid that if he sold out to the Nor'westers and gave them control of the Hudson's Bay Company he was as good as signing an eviction notice for his colonists. So negotiations dragged on late into 1819 with Selkirk slowly, reluctantly coming to the decision to sell. At this point, when the Canadian company was on the verge of clinching a takeover of its British rival, news from the North West completely changed the situation.

The wintering partners of the North West Company were a fractious group. They were, after all, hired for their independence and initiative, not qualities which usually produced reliable "company men." Earlier in the century some had supported Alexander Mackenzie when he broke with the firm's Montreal agents. Now they were restive again. As Colin Robertson had found out during his imprisonment in Fort Chipewyan "the majority of the wintering partners were not on the best terms with the agents, whom they considered the authors of all their misfortunes." A majority may have been an exaggeration but apparently a sizeable number of winterers were indeed falling out with their partners. They were losing patience with the violence and instability of the trade, and they did not understand why the agents could not negotiate some kind of an understanding with the Hudson's Bay Company. Undoubtedly personal intrigues and ambitions were playing their part as well. The dissension came at a particularly awkward time for the North West Company. The partnership agreement which held the company together was coming up for renewal in 1822 and it looked like the firm would break apart. The North West Company could hardly strike a strong bargaining position with the Hudson's Bay Company when it was threatening to disintegrate itself. The dissident winterers were not eager to see the Montreal agents, through their agent in London, Edward Ellice, win control of the Hudson's Bay Company and so in December 1819, they offered to deal directly with the London Committee. This was the news which completely upset the negotiations then going on in England.

During 1820 all three interested parties congregated in London for the final round of talks and after months of negotiations an agreement was finally signed in March 1821. Later William McGillivray would claim: "We have made no submission. We met and negotiated on equal terms." Given that McGillivray's North West Company ceased to exist, his claim seems a peculiar one but there was some truth in it. The Hudson's Bay Company was left in total control of the western fur trade but it was a Hudson's Bay Company different from the one which had existed before the union. Management of the trade was in the hands of a board of directors on which the Nor'westers had equal representation. Profits from the new concern were divided into one hundred shares, twenty-five of which went to North West Company investors and their London agents. The partnership arrangement was abolished and the trade in the Northwest became the responsibility of chief factors and chief traders who were also given a share of the profits. Fifty-three of these positions were created and over half were filled by former Nor'westers. The North West Company was a seriously divided concern when it entered negotiations with the Hudson's Bay Company. It is arguable that it might have ceased to exist anyway in a year's time. Yet it managed to strike a respectable bargain, one which was profitable for its members. McGillivray was right to take some consolation in this accomplishment.

The divisions in the ranks of the North West Company at the time of union were symptomatic of a general weakness in the structure of the company. From the beginning the Canadian concern was a democratic partnership between Montreal merchants and inland traders. Of course men like Simon McTavish and William McGillivray were powerful leaders, but policy decisions were taken by vote at the annual rendezvous and profits were shared among the partners. Initiative was rewarded and not too many questions were asked. The North West Company had to compete with many experienced and determined traders in Montreal and it is doubtful if it could have absorbed them without this sort of flexibility in its organization. If flexibility was the Company's strength, in a crunch it was also its weakness. Profit-sharing left the concern with no reserves of capital to sustain it through an extended period of competition. The Hudson's Bay Company could count on the support of the Bank of England when it got over-extended; the Nor'westers had no financial guardian angel. Furthermore, the independence of its partners left the North West Company without the discipline to choose a policy and act in concert. Historian Richard Glover has called the company a "sprawling, headless octopus. Their tentacles may be everywhere; the directing mind and master hand appear nowhere." As a result, the North West Company in a period of crisis succumbed to its own weaknesses, while the Hudson's Bay Company had the financial resources and managerial discipline to see the contest through.

Writing from Fort William, the site of the final rendezvous of the North West Company in the summer of 1821, William McGillivray lamented that "the fur trade is forever lost to Canada." Many writers have taken up McGillivray's lament and described the merger as a tragedy for the Canadian provinces. But it is really not at all clear what McGillivray might have meant and who exactly should have cared. First of all, in what way was the North West Company Canadian? It had its headquarters in Montreal and for that reason it has been called a Canadian company in this book but most of the partners were Scots and Americans and a lot of the capital came from Britain. True, the bulk of the employees were French Canadian but to call the North West Company Canadian because most of its manpower was French Canadian makes as much sense as calling the Hudson's Bay Company a Scottish company because its servants were Orkneymen. Perhaps McGillivray meant that the union of the companies lost the fur trade to the St. Lawrence River, the spine of the Canadian provinces. If so, he was right. Trade goods now flowed into the Northwest through Hudson Bay exclusively; the *voyageurs'* canoes no longer made the arduous journey to the depot at Fort William each summer. However the contest between these two great geographic possibilities had been settled long before union. Since the turn of the century Nor'westers had recognized the advantages of the Hudson Bay route and the competition had really been over access to this route. If in 1821 it had been the North West Company which had absorbed the Hudson's Bay Company, it would have dropped the St. Lawrence route as quickly as the British Company did. McGillivray's statement also implies that the fur trade was an extremely valuable enterprise for Canadians; but this had not been the case for many years. In the latter half of the eighteenth century the trade had been the most important commercial activity in Quebec and it accounted for three-quarters of all goods exported from the colony. As settlement expanded, however, agriculture occupied a growing number of people, and then after the turn of the century the timber trade enjoyed phenomenal growth until, by 1810, the fur trade accounted for only a small percentage of all exports. It is safe to say that when McGillivray mourned the loss of the fur trade he was mourning for himself and a small group of Montreal merchants, not for Canadians as a whole. For Canadians as a whole the western fur trade had ceased to be a major source of wealth long before the union of 1821.

CHAPTER SEVEN

Losing the Oregon Territory

On September 26, 1824, not long after sunup, a group of fur traders stood on the banks of the La Biche River in northern Alberta looking incredulously up the river in the direction from which they had come the previous day. Someone had just spotted a brigade of canoes bearing down on them; soon enough one of the *voyageurs* recognized the flash of the familiar red paddles and there could no longer be any doubt. Governor George Simpson had made good his boast. He had given them a twenty-day head-start from York Fort and still had caught them before they reached the Rockies. The men stood in embarrassed groups waiting for the governor's arrival and the ridicule which inevitably would follow.

As the new arrivals bumped to a halt in the shallows below the camp, Governor Simpson heaved himself out of one of the canoes and onto the broad back of one of his men who ferried him to dry shore. Coming down to greet him Simpson saw a towering figure of such startling appearance that he recorded his impression in his journal that night: "he was such a figure as I should not like to meet in a dark Night on one of the bye lanes in the neighbourhood of London, dressed in Clothes that had once been fashionable, but now covered with a thousand patches of different Colours, evidently Shewing that he had not lost much time at his Toilette, loaded with Arms and his own herculean dimensions forming a tout ensemble that would convey a good idea of the high way men of former Days."

This was Dr. John McLoughlin, newly appointed chief of the Columbia District, chagrined at being found lingering over his breakfast, coming sheepishly down to greet his superior officer. Together these two men would determine the fortunes of the fur trade across the Rockies for the next two decades. Watching them exchange hellos on the gravel bank that day, the scraggly McLoughlin leaning over the portly, diminutive governor, how many of their men must have wondered just how long two such dissimilar men would be able to work amicably together? How many would have recognized the complete disparity of character which eventually would lead to bitterness and open rebellion?

McLoughlin was very much a man of the New World and the fur trade. Born on a farm near Riviére de Loup to an English-speaking father and a French-Canadian mother, McLoughlin apprenticed as a doctor but was attracted to the western fur country by his uncle, Alexander Fraser, a partner in the North West Company. In the summer of 1803, at the personal invitation of Simon McTavish, McLoughlin signed on with the Montreal company. Most of his early years in the trade were spent around Fort William and though he had second thoughts about the business ("I am sorry I ever came to it," he once wrote) he rose quickly up the ladder to full partnership in the North West Company in 1814. Two years later when violence flared at Red River McLoughlin was right in the thick of things. He was at Fort William when Lord Selkirk and his private army marched west and he was arrested and sent down to Canada for trial. Found not guilty, McLoughlin returned to the Northwest, but he was rapidly losing enthusiasm for the struggle with the Hudson's Bay Company. In 1819 he broke with the management of the North West Company and led a group of disaffected wintering partners in demanding some kind of deal with their British rivals. The next year the dissidents packed him off to London to negotiate directly with the Hudson's Bay Company, and when discussion ended in union McLoughlin was made a chief factor in the new, reorganized Company. So it was a veteran of twenty-one years in the fur trade who welcomed Governor Simpson to his camp that September day, a witness to the furious competition between the North West and XY companies, a participant in all the violence and political manoeuvring which had led to the demise of the Montreal trade.

By comparison, George Simpson was almost a stranger to the fur trade. He had been in the Northwest only four and a half years; his background was the West Indian sugar business. He was younger than McLoughlin and enjoyed neither the other man's physical strength nor his easy familiarity with a trader's life. And yet, in 1824, Simpson was in charge of the Company's northern territory and McLoughlin was his "servant." And in just two more years Simpson would become governor of all the Hudson's Bay Company possessions, the "little emperor" of a domain extending from Labrador to the Pacific, from the plains to the Arctic.

Simpson's success was partly due to connections with the Company's London leadership. Illegitimate by birth, he was lucky enough to have been raised in the home of his grandfather, a Scottish clergyman, where he received a basic education and the security of a stable family life. About 1800, still in his teens, Simpson travelled to London where he went to work for an uncle who was a sugar broker dealing in the West Indies. Not long after, the uncle's firm was joined by Andrew Wedderburn Colville, a Jamaica sugar dealer and brother to the wife of Lord Selkirk. Wedderburn was apparently impressed with young Simpson's work and a few years later, when he and his brother-in-law became influential in the Hudson's Bay Company, Simpson was neatly placed to profit from this confidence.

The future governor was first sent to the Northwest in 1820 as an emissary and an insurance policy. Kidnapping had become an established practise in the trade. Colin Robertson had been held prisoner for a winter at Fort Chipewyan and the committee wanted someone on the scene to take over in the event that William Williams, the chief at York, was abducted. Simpson arrived to learn that Colin Robertson had been kidnapped yet again by the Nor'westers, who this time spirited him out of the country. This left Simpson, the newcomer, no choice but to take over as chief of the Athabasca territory. Despite a career spent exclusively in a London counting house, Simpson proved that winter that he could strut and bluster with the best of them. "The North West Company are not to be put down by Prize fighting," the new trader declared, but even so he tolerated no intimidation from his rivals on Lake Athabasca, who included, he said. "Three Bullies and three noted assassins." The season wore on and the Nor'westers became ever more threatening until finally Simpson, showing he was a fast learner, turned a blind eye and one of his men declared himself to be a constable and arrested the principal troublemaker. That seemed to settle things between the rivals and the rest of the winter passed peaceably enough. Spring found Simpson and his men reduced by hunger and running low on trade goods but confident nevertheless and when he arrived at Grand Rapids to be told about the merger which had just united the two companies Simpson confessed to being disappointed "that instead of a junction our Opponents have not been beaten out of the Field, which with one or two years of good management I am certain might have been effected."

Yet for all his bold pretense at being a fur trader in the buccaneering mould, Simpson's talents were those of the administrator and the bureaucrat and there too lies part of the explanation for his success. He was the right man in the right place at the right time. The war was over, peace had been signed, and the job ahead was that of the diplomat, not the general. Simpson had the advantage of being new to the fur country and uninterested in the squabbles and rivalries which had plagued it for years. His judgement was not soured by bad feeling. He held no grudges himself and was on no one else's enemy list. Personal feeling was secondary to the demands of the trade, to the need for economy after a wasteful period of competition. When decisions were taken no one would accuse him of favouritism or revenge, and so he was able to unify where another might only have antagonized.

Simpson was ideally suited for the job he was given. Even his enemies, and they were many, admitted that he was disarmingly tactful and charming. And from the very beginning it was obvious such qualities were going to be needed. Just because Nor'westers and Hudson Bay men now served the same master did not mean they could forget that only a few seasons before they had been eager to trade blows with their new partners. At the early meetings of the concern, men seated across from each other actually bore scars from their last encounter. "I shall never forget the look of scorn and utter defiance with which they regarded each other the moment their eyes met," recalled one eyewitness. "The highlander's nostrils actually seemed to expand, he snorted, squirted, and spat. . . between his legs and was as restless as if he had been seated on a hillock of ants. . . . I thought it fortunate they were without arms." But in this case as in so many others, "the crafty fox" George Simpson managed to play peacemaker and keep the delicate fabric of the company in one piece.

The new governor was an efficient, even ruthless, administrator. The end of competition gave the committee in London a chance to cut the costs of doing business in the West, and in Simpson it found the perfect instrument of "oeconomy." Wages were slashed; more than half of the men in the service were simply let go; duplicate posts were closed. With regard to the Indians, the new governor was uncompromising and introduced an austerity into the Company's attitude which had not been there before. "I am convinced they must be ruled with a rod of iron," he wrote, "to bring, and Keep them in a proper state of subordination, and the most certain way to effect this is by letting them feel their dependence upon us." These policies were not dreamed up by Simpson but he was in charge of implementing them and he did so with enthusiasm.

As perhaps is evident from his long tenure as overseas governor, Simpson was adept at protecting himself and his decisions from critics both inside and outside the Company. He was able to protect his position by controlling the flow of information from the fur country back to his superiors in Britain. London was a long way from York Factory and the chain of command was direct. Simpson had almost dictatorial powers and it was very difficult for anyone to circumvent him and approach the London committee in person with a grievance. As the years passed and Simpson made himself more and more indispensable, it became less and less likely that London would ever side with one of the common servants against the "little emperor." Simpson used his authority to move men around the fur country like pawns in his own private game of chess. It became obvious that to cross the governor was to risk being transferred next season to some bleak outpost in New Caledonia, or to have your career ruined by a harsh criticism in the next annual letter. Simpson was like a vacuum cleaner as he toured the fur country, sucking up bits of gossip and advice. Always quick to criticize and censure, he was also quick to steal other men's ideas and pass them off as his own, belittling the importance of others so as to secure his own influence. Simpson's well-ordered regime was based on intimidation as well as on sound management principles.

Being new to the trade and to the Northwest, Simpson had a great deal to learn in a short time, and he soon became legendary for his prodigious feats of travel. He was compulsive about going farther faster than anyone had ever gone before, taking malicious delight in overtaking travellers who had left before him, swooping down on them from behind, as he did to Dr. McLoughlin. Simpson was shrewd enough to know that displays of courage and endurance were the way to win respect from the veteran traders and so he drove himself and his men harder than was necessary. A day with the governor's brigade began in darkness about 2:00 A.M. After six hours of paddling, there was a break for breakfast, then back into the canoes until 1:00 P.M. when a ten-minute luncheon halt was called. About 8:00 P.M. the weary travellers camped for the night; the day's voyaging had lasted eighteen hours and had covered as many as a hundred and fifty kilometres.

Simpson enjoyed the outward symbols of his powerful position. His canoe was well stocked with ham, butter, cheese, port wine, and Madeira, as well as the usual pemmican and hard biscuit. At times he travelled with piper and bugler and when he approached the various posts, his arrival was advertised like that of some European prince. "As we waft along under easy sail," recalled one of his fellow travellers, "the men with a clean change and mounting new feathers, the Highland bagpipes in the Governor's canoe, was echoed by the bugle in mine; then these were laid aside, on nearer approach to port, to give free scope to the vocal organs of about eighteen Canadians (French) to chant one of those *voyageur* airs peculiar to them. . . . Immediately on landing, His Excellency was preceded by the piper from the water to the Fort. . . ." One can imagine the mixture of dread and awe which would greet the governor at these simple log huts in the wilderness when he descended on them.

It was a more subdued party which joined Dr. McLoughlin and his men that day in 1824. The governor was content to impress with his speed alone, and anyway, he and the Doctor had parted less than a month before. From this point they would travel together, the governor condescending to slow his pace so that McLoughlin could keep up. It is tempting to imagine what the two men talked about as they made their way across the Rockies and down to the mouth of the Columbia. Any discussion of politics would soon have foundered. Simpson's politics matched his personality — restrained, conservative, and a little cold-hearted. He despised radicals of any kind, which gave him an excuse to dislike the United States, a country he called "an asylum for the outcasts and malcontents of all Nations." McLoughlin, on the other hand, styled himself as just one of those malcontents. In 1838, for instance, he would openly avow his sympathy for the *patriote* rebels in Lower Canada. No wonder an irritated Simpson later described him as "a great stickler for rights and privileges and sets himself up for a righter of wrongs . . . would be a Radical in any Country — under any Government and under any circumstances."

If politics was too contentious, perhaps the travellers talked of women and sex. It was a topic often enough on the governor's mind at least. He had left two illegitimate children behind him when he had first come to Rupert's Land, and after only two years in the country he wrote to a friend: "I suspect my name will become as notorious as the late Govr. in regard to plurality of wives." But here again the two men shared little common ground. Like most veteran fur traders, McLoughlin had married a mixed-blood woman, a fact for which he saw no need to apologize. His marriage lasted until his death and apparently he did not discriminate against other native women. On one occasion a particularly obnoxious Christian missionary was spreading malicious gossip about McLoughlin's wife in official letters back to London. Enraged, the Doctor laid into him with his walking stick, beating him about the head and shoulders and threatening to kill him until he was pulled away. For his part, Simpson was not overly concerned about the reputation of his country wives. Indian and mixed-blood women were for him conveniences to be enjoyed then discarded. During his first year in the country, he kept a young mixed-blood, Betsey Sinclair, "at bed and board" in Athabasca and she bore him his first North American child, a daughter. But when he was appointed governor he deserted the two of them, writing callously to a friend at York: "My Family concerns I leave entirely to your kind management, if you can dispose of the Lady it will be satisfactory as she is an unnecessary and expensive appendage, I see no fun in keeping a Woman without enjoying her charms which my present rambling Life does not enable me to do; but if she is unmarketable I have no wish that she be a general accommodation shop to all the young bucks at the Factory and in addition to her own chastity a padlock may be useful. . . ." Over the next few years Simpson had at least two other mistresses whom he referred to contemptuously as his "bits of brown" or his "commodities." Finally, when he decided it was time to take a wife, the governor left his latest mistress, Margaret Taylor, then pregnant with his child, and returned to England where he married his cousin, seventeen-year-old Frances Simpson. When the governor and his lady returned to Rupert's Land, Margaret was kept discreetly out of the way, and the next year a marriage was arranged with someone else. Frances Simpson was kept in the dark about her husband's previous liaisons and his brood of mixed-blood children, but she had her suspicions and, as a friend recorded, "she was always terrified to look about her in case of seeing something disagreeable." Simpson's racism and flippant callousness were extreme even for his time. They would not have struck a sympathetic chord with Dr. McLoughlin and it is safe to assume the two men did not spend much time sharing sexual exploits.

In all probability, Simpson and McLoughlin spent the journey to the Columbia talking business. There was, after all, a good deal to discuss. The Hudson's Bay Company had inherited the fur trade country west of the Rockies from the North West Company when the two concerns joined forces. Its boundaries were very much in question, crowded by Russians on the north and Americans on the south, and the trade itself had stagnated for several years. Following on the explorations of Simon Fraser and David Thompson, the North West Company set up a chain of posts in the region, anchored at the mouth of the Columbia by Fort George. But success was frustrated by problems of supply, and by regulations which hampered the China trade.

In 1821, shortly after the amalgamation of the two fur companies, the British Parliament gave the Crown the right to grant trading licenses in North America. As a reward for resolving the troublesome competition which was disrupting affairs in Rupert's Land, the Hudson's Bay Company received a monopoly applying to its original chartered territory, plus Athabasca and the so-called Oregon Territory as well. This put the Columbia firmly in the Company's domain and made it part of the reorganization which was being carried out all over the Northwest. For some time Simpson had been hearing disquieting rumours about waste and mismanagement on the Columbia. This was why he was taking the trouble to venture across the continent and also why an experienced hand like John McLoughlin was appointed to take charge of the district.

The Hudson's Bay Company on the Columbia was venturing into a political void. Prior to 1803 the western border of the United States had been the Mississippi River. Beyond lay the Louisiana territory, owned by Spain and little known to traders and explorers. In 1803 the Americans and the Spanish concluded the Louisiana Purchase which handed over the vast tract beyond the Mississippi to the United States. However, it was generally agreed that the Louisiana territory extended westward only as far as the crest of the Rockies. Beyond that point, along the coastal strip of the continent, Spanish, British, Russians, and Americans all pressed their claims. The United States had established an honest claim to the region of the Columbia River. Its mouth had been found in 1792 by an American trader, and later another American, John Jacob Astor, had sent an expedition to establish a settlement on the spot. During the War of 1812, under threat of British cannon, Astor's traders sold their post to the North West Company, but after the war an American ship arrived back at the river to conduct a brief flag-raising ceremony, just to serve notice that Washington had not lost interest. In 1818 Britain and the United States actually sat down at the bargaining table to settle the issue. The Americans proposed that the forty-ninth parallel would be a suitable boundary between their possessions and the British ones, since it was already an accepted boundary across the middle of the continent. But the British saw no reason to concede the Columbia. It was, they argued, an important artery of the fur trade, a trade created and dominated by British subjects. They wanted the river to represent the border.

An interesting sidelight to the 1818 negotiations was a proposal made at the last minute by one of the Americans, Albert Gallatin. In search of compromise, Gallatin suggested the border should follow the forty-ninth parallel westward from the mountains, intersect the Columbia, but then dip southward before reaching the Pacific so that the Puget Sound area and the rivers draining into it would be left in British hands. The American proposal was based on a gigantic misunderstanding. According to a map, which was believed by both parties to be reputable, a large river with its source far to the north in New Caledonia emptied into Puget Sound somewhere south of the forty-ninth parallel, between the Fraser and the Columbia. This river, called the Caledonia, would belong to the British under the terms of the new proposal and the Americans naturally thought it would be adequate compensation for the loss of the Columbia. The River Caledonia, of course, did not exist, though this was not confirmed for several years. It may well be that the map which showed it so clearly was a fake, drawn up by the North West Company to mislead the diplomats and win a boundary favourable to its own interests. If the imaginary river had been settled on as the international border, the valuable harbours of Puget Sound and the modern city of Seattle might well be part of Canada today. As it turned out, the ruse, if that is what it was, was only partly successful. The river was taken as fact, but the British rejected Gallatin's proposal anyway and negotiations ended in stalemate. Instead of a firm boundary, the two countries agreed to joint occupancy for a period of ten years, at the end of which time they would try again. This was the situation the Hudson's Bay Company inherited when it began trading in the territory.

As George Simpson descended on the Pacific Coast in 1824, trailing Dr. McLoughlin in his wake, he passed by the interior posts and quickly formed an opinion about the state of the district. "Everything appears to me on the Columbia on too extended a scale except the Trade," he pronounced. "Mismanagement and extravagance has been the order of the day." Settled into Fort George for the winter, he set about hacking and pruning with his usual enthusiasm. Straight away the complement of men should be cut almost in half, he recommended, a move which would shave about £2000 from the company's wage bill alone. Those who remained should have their style of living radically reduced. According to Simpson, servants were depending too heavily on provisions imported from Europe, at great expense, and neglecting local food sources. The Governor served notice that the company would be cutting back on imports. In the future men would be expected to hunt and fish for more of their food. As well, vegetable gardens and farming ventures would be encouraged. "It has been said that Farming is no branch of the Fur Trade," he wrote, "but I consider that every pursuit tending to lighten the Expense of the Trade is a branch thereof...." While his own men were encouraged to be more self-sufficient, the Indians were to be encouraged in the opposite direction. In all ways the Indians should "imbibe our manners and customs and imitate us in Dress," taught the governor, "our Supplies would thus become necessary to them which would increase the consumption of European produce and manufactures and in like measure increase and benefit our trade...."

Simpson knew that the joint occupancy agreement with the United States would be running out soon and no matter what agreement followed, it was highly unlikely that the British would have a claim to any territory south of the Columbia. It seemed sensible, therefore, to shift the company's headquarters from Fort George, situated on the south side of the river, to a more diplomatically defensible position on the opposite shore. The next spring work began on Fort Vancouver on the banks of the river several kilometres from its mouth. This remained the headquarters of the Columbia trading district until the company evacuated in the 1840s.

In the short run Simpson was more concerned about American free traders than he was about diplomats and boundary negotiations. For several years venturesome Yankees had been feeling their way along the upper tributaries of the Missouri River, seeking the safest and most direct routes into the Rocky Mountains from the Great Western Plain. By the mid-1820s they had arrived among the frigid streams and alpine meadows of the central Rockies where they inaugurated a new kind of trapping system. Fall, winter, and spring, nomadic trappers scoured the valleys for beaver, living in isolated camps in tents half buried in the snow and moving about on horseback or by foot. These were the legendary Mountain Men, men like Jedediah Smith and Bill Sublette, who opened many of the passes through the mountains while stripping the region bare of beaver and carrying on a running guerrilla war with the Indians. In the summer they would gather at the rendezvous in some central river valley with their suppliers from the east and for several weeks engage in a prolonged and drunken carouse. When Simpson arrived on the Columbia this undisciplined pack of free traders, these "people of the worst character, run-aways from Jails, and outcasts from Society," as the Governor called them, were tumbling down out of the mountains toward Oregon and the Hudson's Bay Company territory.

As a head-on collision loomed, more was at stake than a few animal pelts. At least Simpson thought so. He recognized that the greatest threat to Hudson's Bay Company control of Oregon was the settler. If "foreign" settlers could be kept out of the district, the trade could flourish in remote obscurity. American trappers were, Simpson believed, the leading edge of settlement and had to be stopped in their tracks and driven from the country. What was at issue, then, was the fate of a large chunk of the Company's empire.

To combat the encroaching Americans, Simpson planned a scorched earth policy. In other parts of the fur country the Hudson's Bay Company was trying to conserve the dwindling stocks of beaver, but Simpson decided that the territory north of the Columbia would be protected by a virtual fur desert, a *cordon sanitaire* in which fur-bearing animals would be ruthlessly exterminated. "The country is a rich preserve of Beaver," the governor noted, "and which for political reasons we should endeavour to destroy as fast as possible." Since the opposition would be unable to find furs in this depleted area, they would presumably not bother venturing beyond it.

The focus of the Company's policy was the Snake River Country to the south and east of the Columbia. The Snake was a treacherous, unnavigable river, rising in the Rocky Mountains and winding about sixteen hundred kilometres across southern Idaho before meeting the Columbia in southeast Washington state. North West Company traders had begun making forays into the valley of the Snake in 1818, and when the Hudson's Bay Company took over, the assault on the Snake country stepped up. Simpson chose Peter Skene Ogden to lead the expeditions.

As a young man Ogden had earned a reputation as one of the most notorious of the North West Company bullies. The son of a Quebec judge, he was not restrained by respect for the law or fair trading practices. Along with his lifelong friend Sam Black, Ogden thrived on beating up rival traders, cutting their fish nets, slashing their canoes, stealing their furs. On one occasion he may have murdered an Indian who balked at trading with him. Eventually he was spirited across the mountains to the Columbia to avoid arrest. His own comrades found him a lively companion; "the humorous, honest, eccentric, law-defying Peter Ogden," one of them called him, "the terror of the Indians, and the delight of all gay fellows," but, not unnaturally, at the merger of the two fur companies Ogden was not invited to join the Hudson's Bay

Company. However, he went to London to plead his case, and in 1823 he was welcomed back into the trade and sent out to the Pacific coast to lead the Snake River expeditions.

The Snake River country was the Siberia of the Pacific fur trade. Eleven months of the year the brigade risked hostile Indians, starvation, and exposure in remote, snowbound valleys. Game was often scarce; so was grass for the pack horses. On one particularly awful expedition far to the south the horses died for lack of food and the starving trappers fed on their carcasses and drank their blood to survive. "This life makes a young man sixty in a few years," wrote Ogden. The men were principally trappers, not traders; they caught the beaver themselves instead of trading from the Indians. Wading knee deep in the glacial streams, they set metal traps on the gravel bottoms and baited them with overhanging willow sticks rubbed with castoreum, a smelly, oily liquid obtained from the beaver's sex glands. When a beaver stepped in the trap trying to reach the willow, the jaws snapped shut, and, as it struggled into deeper water to escape, the animal was dragged down by the weight and drowned. As many as seventy-five men went with each expedition, too large a force for the Hudson's Bay Company to provide, and the ranks were filled with free trappers, drifters from the East, mixed-bloods, and Iroquois, who wandered into this country so far from civilization for reasons of their own and joined up as the only way of making a living. They earned quite a reputation for themselves. "The very scum of the earth," cried George Simpson; "discordant headstrong ill-designing set of rascals," was the opinion of another Company officer. And yet Company policy had much to do with the free trappers' unreliability. They were not salaried employees, but instead took equipment and supplies from the Company and paid for them with the furs they collected. The Company cleared a tidy profit charging inflated prices for its goods and giving low prices for the pelts. It took Ogden only one season to recognize that it was resentment at this exploitation that made the Snake River trappers so hard to manage and the policy was changed.

As the years passed, the term, *Snake River Country* was loosely applied to all the territory covered by Peter Skene Ogden during his six expeditions between 1824 and 1830; it covered a vast tract of land stretching from the banks of the Columbia to the Rockies, to the southeast as far as the Great Salt Lake, and to the south as far as the Gulf of California. Each year Ogden brought back thousands of pelts, and by the time he retired from the Snake River his expeditions had killed as many as twenty thousand beaver. Against such spirited enterprise the Americans could not get a foothold, and by the 1830s the Hudson's Bay Company had complete mastery of the fur trade in the Oregon.

The fur trade in the Pacific Northwest in practise consisted of two fur trades. In the interior of New Caledonia and along the Columbia River, traders lived in log posts and collected furs from the Indians in the conventional manner. This was the trade dominated by the Hudson's Bay Company. But along the coast of what is now British Columbia, there was another kind of trade, carried on each summer from sailing ships cruising the inlets and harbours to barter for sea otter skins. This coastal trade began in the 1780s and came to be dominated by American sea captains. Initially the Hudson's Bay Company took no interest in it, but this indifference changed with the arrival of Simpson and McLoughlin and plans were made to establish a string of posts along the Pacific shore.

The Company was not alone in wanting to grab a share of the coastal trade. In the north, Russian traders were casting covetous glances southward from their headquarters at Sitka. In 1821 the Russian government announced that it was claiming the entire coast as far down as the top of Vancouver Island. This claim was a little far-fetched, since the Russians had no settlements along this strip of coast, and the British were able to convince the Russians to abandon their interest in the coast below latitude 54'40°.

With the Russians out of the way, the Hudson's Bay Company mounted its own campaign to drive Americans from the region. Posts were built at the mouths of the Fraser, Nass, and Skeena rivers, and ships were brought in to supply the posts and trade along the coast as well. The strategy was considered essential to deny the Americans access to furs coming down from the interior as well as to the sea otter trade. And it worked. By the mid-1830s the Hudson's Bay Company had extended its domination of the Pacific Northwest to include the coastal trade.

John McLoughlin ruled over this domain from his arrival in 1824 to his retirement in 1845. During these twenty-one years the country north of the Columbia was indisputably British territory. In the 1840s there were less than a dozen American settlers in the entire area and no American enterprise. At the same time, under McLoughlin's direction, about a thousand British subjects occupied the region, trading for furs, farming hundreds of acres of cleared land, and raising substantial herds of livestock. And yet, ironically, despite the fact that he was born in Quebec and spent all his life working for British-Canadian companies in British territory, McLoughlin is remembered today as the "Father of Oregon." In the crunch, his success and the success of the Company were irrelevent to the larger requirements of manifest destiny and international diplomacy. And so, in 1846, the Hudson's Bay Company retreated north of the forty-ninth parallel and the Columbia was handed over to the United States.

The writing had been on the wall since 1827. In that year Britain and the United States renewed their agreement of joint occupancy, having once again failed to settle on a permanent boundary. But the Americans realized that the Columbia was theirs whenever they wanted to push the matter hard enough. As Albert Gallatin, the American negotiator, noted prophetically, ". . . Great Britain does not seem indisposed to let the country gradually and silently slide into the hands of the United States. . . ." The British quite simply had no great interest in this remote land of mountains and forest. The fur trade was its only value and that was not a good enough reason to sour international relations and run the risk of war. The British would put up a bold front; they would not give in to threats or appear to be chased out; but they did not care enough to go the distance with the Americans. In a sense the Hudson's Bay Company was also responsible for the loss of its own territory. It had long been a truism that fur trade and settlement did not mix. As a result the Company was reluctant to welcome colonists into their trading areas and liked to keep strict control over their movements. In the Columbia the Company refused to sell land to settlers, leasing it instead and demanding a share of the farmer's produce. These feudal requirements naturally discouraged immigration and kept the population of the Columbia low. It is possible that if a large population of British colonists had occupied the Columbia, the British government might have felt more inclined to hold on to it and western Washington state might be part of British Columbia today.

After being shuffled aside for almost thirty years the "Oregon Question" came to a head in 1844. Stricken by "Oregon Fever," Americans were becoming increasingly expansionist, and that fall elected a new president, James K. Polk, who campaigned under the "All Oregon" banner. "All Oregon" meant every bit of British-held territory on the Pacific coast, all the way to latitude 54'40°; in other words, most of what is now British Columbia.

For several years American settlers on the Willamette River, not far from the present site of Portland, Oregon, had been wanting Washington to take over their colony. In 1843 they formed their own government and clamoured to be absorbed into the United States. In Congress a group of expansionist hardliners contemplated war if Britain did not clear out of the Columbia immediately. Polk raised the temperature of "Oregon Fever" when in his inaugural address to the nation he stated that his country's claim to Oregon was "clear and unquestionable" and that it was inevitable that Americans should bring the "blessings of self-government" to the area. But it is not at all certain that Polk, for all his noisy rhetoric, really believed in the "All Oregon" cause; he may have been merely establishing a bargaining position. It certainly looked that way when, shortly after taking office, the new president made an offer to establish the forty-ninth parallel as Oregon's northern border.

The British had already come to accept that this was the best they could do in terms of territory, but they hoped as well to gain some assurances about navigation on the Columbia River. Because Polk's offer made no mention of this, the British negotiator in Washington felt justified in rejecting it out of hand without even referring to London for instructions. When his superiors found out what he had done they immediately urged Polk to resubmit the proposal for discussion. But the president, stunned at the rebuff, reverted to a more aggressive position and asked Congress to end the joint occupancy agreement so that "the national rights in Oregon" could be "firmly maintained."

Britain was not going to be bullied out of the Columbia and events seemed to be spiralling towards war. Yet war was not really likely; neither side wanted it. The British believed that Oregon was, in the words of one leading politician, "of such insignificant value as not to compensate the losses and miseries that one single month of war must produce." As for the American government, it preferred to settle the issue peacefully so it could attend to its other expansionist claims in Texas. It was a matter of placating the jingoist factions on both sides and reaching an accommodation in the middle ground. In 1846 the forty-ninth parallel was again proposed as a boundary, this time by the British and this time without strings attached. Polk acted promptly to turn the proposal into a treaty and the "Oregon Question" was settled.

The Oregon Treaty was a diplomatic setback for Great Britain. The United States got the territory it wanted: the British got nothing. But the treaty was largely irrelevant to the fur trade. Returns from the Columbia district were in sharp decline anyway and three years before the treaty the Hudson's Bay Company had built Fort Victoria at the southern tip of Vancouver Island, secure from the vagaries of boundary disputes. When the Company evacuated the Columbia, Fort Victoria became its Pacific head-quarters, the spot where the declining years of the fur trade on the Pacific slope were orchestrated. As it turned out, the loss of Oregon was a loss for Canada, denying any possibility that the valuable coastal harbours of Washington state would be part of the new confederation just two decades away. But as far as the fur trade was concerned, it was already finished with the Columbia.

There was one old servant who did not make the move to Victoria. By 1846 John McLoughlin had left the Company. His departure was not voluntary. He was not fired exactly, but his position was made untenable enough that resignation was his only option. After a quarter of a century of service, McLoughlin left the Company in disgrace, a pathetic figure, sloughed off like some embarrassing relative who won't shut up about the family skeletons. How did such a distinguished career end in such ignominy?

McLoughlin and his governor, George Simpson, were never in complete accord about the far western trade. After his initial visit in 1824 Simpson made only two more trips to the Columbia, but the business there was very much under his thumb, and McLoughlin was often embroiled with him over differences of opinion about trading strategy. McLoughlin did not like to prosecute the coastal trade from ships, preferring the permanence of posts; Simpson preferred the opposite. McLoughlin thought steamships, which the Company started using on the coast in 1836, troublesome and unnecessary; Simpson thought the opposite. McLoughlin tried to treat openly with American settlers and traders, hoping to win their business for the Company; Simpson wanted them driven from the country. On all these matters McLoughlin was listened to, then overruled. "It is perfectly out of the question to talk of discussion," he complained, "when there are only two persons at the discussion, and one has the power to decide as he pleases and does." The Doctor did as he was ordered but he was not a man who took orders easily. By all accounts he had a volatile temper and an argumentative nature. He was usually involved in a running feud with someone. As the grudges against Simpson multiplied, McLoughlin's resentment grew until finally it exploded.

Simpson arrived on the Columbia in 1841 on his way around the world. He stayed long enough to irritate McLoughlin by closing down some coastal posts without consulting him, then departed for Hawaii. In April of the next year the governor was back on the coast sailing for Alaska when he stopped in at Fort Stikine. This remote post at the mouth of the Stikine River was under the direction of John McLoughlin Junior, the Chief Factor's mixed-blood son. Simpson arrived to discover that the young trader had been murdered by his own men just a few days before. The Governor immediately launched an inquiry and allowed himself to be convinced, on the testimony of the men involved, that young McLoughlin had been a heavy drinker and a tyrannical leader who was killed by one of his servants in self-defense. Showing the "cold and callous heart" he was often accused of having, the governor wrote to the Doctor at Fort Vancouver to tell him that his son had been slain "in a drunken fray" and that "the whole conduct and management of Mr. McLoughlin was exceedingly bad, and his violence when under the influence of liquor, which was very frequently the case, amounting to insanity." The letter contained no condolences, no regrets, just a sustained criticism of the dead man's conduct.

Simpson's attitude was fueled by his animosity toward natives generally. The racism he expressed about Indians carried over into his feelings about the mixed-bloods. He thought they were shiftless, stupid, conceited, too close to a depraved state of nature to be useful to the Company in any but the lower positions. In the case of John McLoughlin Junior, this stereotype must have been confirmed in his mind by what he knew of the young man's troubled history. John Junior was born at Rainy Lake to McLoughlin's mixed-blood wife, the daughter of a fur trader. As a boy he lived with his great-uncle, a doctor, at Terrebonne in Lower Canada. When he came of age there were no positions open in the fur trade, the natural calling for someone of his background, so the elder McLoughlin sent the boy to France to study medicine. Initially young John did well but then some incident occurred which brought him home in disgrace. In Montreal, despite his father's attempts to have him pick up his medical studies, John Junior loafed about piling up debts. In 1836 he joined a bizarre expedition led by an American adventurer, James Dickson, who styled himself Montezuma II and was planning to lead an "Indian Liberation Army" of natives to the western United States, where he intended turning California into a kingdom of Indians ruled over by himself. This expedition travelled first to Red River to find recruits and when it got there George Simpson decided to undermine it by wooing away some of its leaders. John Junior was one of these and when Simpson offered him a job with the Company he accepted. He was sent out to the Columbia to be with his father and apparently did well, but

Simpson nevertheless must have retained an impression of an unstable, untrustworthy "half-breed" and so it did not take him long to form his opinion of events at Fort Stikine.

Dr. McLoughlin, of course, was furious at the way his son's death was treated. The John Junior described by Simpson was not the John Junior his father knew. That young man was not bad-tempered, was not cruel, was not incompetent, was not an alcoholic, was not any of the things he now stood accused of being. What's more, the Doctor was told that he should accept Simpson's version of events and forget the whole affair for the good of the Company. But McLoughlin was not a man to stay quiet in the face of a monumental injustice. "I will do all I can to Investigate this to me most painful affair," he warned London, "so as to ascertain the truth and that justice may take its course."

McLoughlin did not have to wait long for fresh evidence to come to hand. Soon after the affair a servant named Pierre Kanaquassé, who had been at Fort Stikine, came forward and admitted that the story Simpson was told, and believed, was a fabrication. According to Kanaquassé, young McLoughlin was murdered because he would not allow his men either to have Indian women into their rooms or to leave the post at night themselves. The men commonly stole items from the company stores to give to their native mistresses, said Kanaquassé, and the post master punished them with good reason. The murder was apparently not a spur of the moment "accident." It was carefully planned — and not even the first attempt made on McLoughlin's life; Kanaquassé admitted to having made three tries himself. Along with Kanaquassé's testimony the elder McLoughlin added other evidence until he was able to refute the Simpson version on almost all points. There was no question now that his son was the victim of a cold-blooded murder, carried out by a gang of brutish servants who afterwards conspired to conceal the truth. John Junior was not an immoderate drinker, and by all trustworthy accounts he treated his men as fairly as they deserved and died trying to do his best by the Company's affairs.

But McLoughlin was destined never to get satisfaction. It made no difference that he had ferreted out the truth, or that the committee in London apparently agreed that Simpson had been wrong. The Company could not afford to admit that some of its men were brutal murderers and that its chief officer had been completely taken in by them. Simpson was indispensible, McLoughlin was not. The Company was not about to contradict and embarrass its top man in Rupert's Land for the sake of rescuing the reputation of a minor post master — and a mixed-blood at that. No one was prosecuted for the murder and the whole matter was dropped. At least, the London committee wanted it dropped. But McLoughlin didn't.

He continued to bombard headquarters with defenses of his son, with new evidence, with attacks on Simpson, who he now held personally responsible for the fact that John Junior had been left alone in command of a group of such rough hands. Simpson never did recant; it was not in his nature to do so. He refused to admit that he was wrong and two years after the murder he wrote to the Doctor, in very condescending tones, that "through the whole of this painful business you have, naturally, I admit, but unadvisedly, sacrificed your judgement to your feelings." From Simpson's point of view this was, after all, a minor affair. He had an empire to manage. Meanwhile, as McLoughlin's accusations became more shrill, the committee became more impatient. It was an impossible situation. McLoughlin could not be allowed to go on libelling the governor. He was forcing the Company to come down on the side of one man or the other and in that contest there could be only one winner.

In 1845 McLoughlin finally gave up. His policies were under attack and he had been replaced as chief of the Columbia District by a three-man Board of Management. As well, he had suffered a great personal loss when he learned that his son-in-law had committed suicide in California. Depressed, and deeply offended at his treatment by the Company, the Doctor resigned from the service. "Gentlemen," he wrote, "I will serve you no longer." He moved to a piece of land at Oregon City on the Willamette where he became a mill operator and an American citizen. He died at age seventy-three in 1857.

The feud between John McLoughlin and George Simpson was a clash of contrary personalities. But it was also a clash of styles that threw into bold relief the differences between the fur trade in its early and late phases. McLoughlin was a rough trader; tough, physically imposing, irascible, emblematic of the men who went west during the highly competitive years when a trader had to be strong enough to intimidate his opponent, wily enough to out-manoeuvre him and knowledgeable enough about the Indians to out-trade him. Trained to a profession, often dispirited by isolation and loneliness, the Doctor nevertheless adapted to the culture of the western country and to the land itself. He took a native wife; he shed refined habits and eastern clothes and cultivated a wild appearance; he even settled there when time came to retire. If McLoughlin was the rough-edged frontiersman, Simpson was the smooth administrator suited to the new era of monopoly which followed the merger of 1821. Just as the trade now had to make less compromises with the native people, so Simpson made less compromises with the country he came from England to govern. He detested the local people. He married a white woman and tried to create a replica of genteel English society at Red River. His skills, and they were considerable, were managerial skills. He prided himself on efficiency and economy, qualities not always prized by early traders. They relied on force of personality, and physical intimidation to manage their men; Simpson was backed by the authority of a powerful company. He was a careerist and an opportunist in ways his predecessors could not have contemplated. He functioned in a different kind of administrative structure and he learned to use it to advantage. It is tempting to see in the differences between McLoughlin and Simpson a struggle between the old order and the new in the western fur country.

CHAPTER EIGHT

The New Regime: "A Strife of Blood"

When the Hudson's Bay Company found itself alone in the field following merger with its longtime rival in 1821, the London Committee quickly began to exploit the advantages of a monopoly position. Economies were made in all aspects of the business, excesses were abolished, and Indian trappers began to feel the lash of restraint. After this brief period of adjustment, however, the trade settled into a routine for the most part undisturbed by major changes for several decades. The storm of competition was followed by the relative calm of monopoly. At the same time a unique society was developing in the Canadian West, a society which combined, often comically, the gentility of Victorian Britain with the awkwardness of the American frontier. The image we often have of the West at this time is of a wild, primitive place, populated by picturesque natives, which was not "civilized" until the arrival of immigrant farmers late in the nineteenth century. But like so many images Canadians have of themselves, this one is false. The West did not need taming; it had already been occupied by the advance guard of European civilization.

First to feel the effects of the new austerity were the men who worked in the fur trade. During the competitive period they enjoyed some bargaining power with their employers but this advantage disappeared with the North West Company and the men could do little when the new Company slashed salaries as much as thirty per cent. They could always quit, of course, and some did, but not many veterans of the fur country were suited to making a living in Canada or Britain, especially with mixed-blood wives and children to support. Many men were not given a choice; the Company cut its workforce by about two-thirds and the elderly, the infirm, and the unruly were simply let go as their contracts expired. For these men the reverse side of "oeconomy" was uncertainty and hardship. The Company recognized that it was in its own best interest to extend some help to dispossessed servants. "These people form a burden which cannot be got rid of without expense," London officials reasoned, "and if allowed to remain in their present condition, they will become dangerous to the Peace of the Country and the safety of the Trading Posts." Instead, unemployed servants and their families were offered free passage to the colony at Red River where they were settled on small farms and given the necessaries to get themselves established.

At this time Red River was developing into the administrative and social centre of the fur trade country. Certainly it was the only settlement of any size in the Northwest, numbering over five thousand residents by 1850. The core of the community were the Kildonan Scots left over from the original migration sponsored by Lord Selkirk. They were farmers and herdsmen and seldom brushed up against the fur trade. Distantly related to these settlers were the mixed-blood veterans of the Hudson's Bay Company, offspring of Indian wives and Orkney servants, who had retired to the colony rather than leave the country. Mixed in with these English-speakers were a small group of Saulteaux and Cree families who had abandoned their traditional way of life to become farmers, and a group of French Canadians clustered around the Catholic mission at St. Boniface. And lastly there were Red River's most important residents, the Métis; the French-speaking, Catholic mixed-bloods who played such a crucial role in the history of the Northwest. The Métis were a unique social entity, identifying with neither French nor Indian culture. They saw themselves as a people apart, a "new nation" with its own ethnic identity and its own lifestyle. For the most part the Métis lived on narrow farms running back from the river banks. Their farming, however, was subsistence at best, and the people relied for their living on the much more adventurous buffalo hunt. Each spring and fall a long parade of Red River carts wound out from the settlement across the prairie in search of the herds of bison. As many as twelve hundred carts took part, returning with over five hundred thousand kilograms of pemmican to sell to the fur traders. But the Métis derived more than a livelihood from the hunt; they also developed a set of laws, a unique political organization, and their own status system. It was in the hunt that the Métis forged their sense of cultural separateness which they would assert so tragically in the years ahead.

Once the Company had thinned its ranks of what it considered "deadwood," it began to fill them again with men more suitable to the trade, chosen according to a strategy carefully thought out by George Simpson. In the past the Hudson's Bay Company had depended on the Orkney Islands for servants. The governor, however, did not like relying on a single source for manpower. For one thing, a workforce divided by ethnic rivalry was not likely to find the unity necessary to challenge the Company over wages and working conditions. For another, each group had characteristics which had to be carefully balanced. Simpson valued French Canadians for their experience, their endurance, and their relative docility, while he knew that Orkneymen had the advantage of being willing to sign on for low wages. Other Scotsmen and the Irish were of doubtful value, he thought, "quarrelsome, independent, and inclined to form leagues and cabals," and mixed-blood youths were proud and unreliable. The result was a labour force filled with a calculated mix of Canadians and Islanders leavened with a few Scots and Irishmen. This policy was amended through the years as British servants became harder to attract and native mixed-bloods became too convenient to ignore. Red River was proving a difficult place to make a living. Other than the buffalo hunt, which was only seasonal, the colony was isolated from markets for its produce and had limited arable land for farming. The Company was pretty well the only employer and by the 1850s mixed-bloods formed the single largest group of servants.

Employment in the fur country was complicated by the seasonal nature of the work. In a real sense the Hudson's Bay Company was a great collection agency and transport company. It gathered up furs from all across the Northwest, carried them down the rivers and streams to Hudson Bay, and shipped them across the Atlantic to European fur markets. Because of the climate in Rupert's Land, most of this could only be done during a brief period each summer, which meant that the Company's manpower needs were much greater then than at any other time. Since it made no sense to carry a permanent workforce large enough to handle only seasonal work, the Company began to make more and more use of temporary labour, Indian and mixed-blood casuals who hired on for the busy season to man boats and canoes and to ship cargo. This trend heralded the development of a free labour market in the West in which men were hired for wages as they were needed and did not look to a paternalistic company for food, clothing, and shelter.

Equally hard hit by the new austerity imposed by the Hudson's Bay Company were the Indian trappers who supplied the furs. For years they had played one set of traders off against the other, extracting liberal presents of tobacco and liquor and otherwise enjoying the courtship of the rivals. It was competition which allowed natives to manipulate the terms of trade and retain some control over their own destinies. After 1821 the Indians' ability to affect the trade was severely limited. Although prices offered for furs actually went up "to prevent the Indians from desponding under the idea that they will suffer from the total absence of competition," presents were eliminated, credit reduced, and furs refused if they were not marketable or in season. Liquor was removed from the list of trade goods and by late in the 1820s alcoholic imports had fallen to about one-twelfth of what they had been in former times. Worried about depletion of the beaver, the Company also encouraged conservation of the animal. These measures could not be applied with equal vigour across the fur country. In border areas, where American free traders were accessible, the Company still had to bend to Indian demands. Likewise on the plains, where the people remained largely indifferent to European trade articles, liquor remained an indispensable article of trade for meat supplies. Still, in the wooded areas where they relied heavily on imported goods, Indians were less able to resist the demands of the Hudson's Bay Company. For them the end of competition meant a reduction in bargaining power and a consequent reduction in cultural independence.

The Plains Indians — the Cree, Assiniboine, and Blackfoot — continued to supply traders with the pemmican which formed such an essential part of their diet. But for the most part, these people played out their own tragic destiny separate from the fur trade. During the first half of the nineteenth century the Plains Indians were embroiled in a complicated system of alliances and warfare. Generally speaking, the Cree and Assiniboine were allied against the Sioux, Mandan, and Blackfoot. At bottom the warfare was about horses: the Cree and Assiniboine wanted them and the others had them, or at least controlled access to them. Horses were an essential part of Plains culture and since Euro-Canadian traders did not supply them, they remained of peripheral interest to the native people.

Two things happened towards the middle of the century to reduce the independence of the Plains people. One was another smallpox epidemic.

In the summer of 1837 infection was carried up the Missouri River from St. Louis on board a supply boat belonging to the American Fur Company. As Indians from the north came in to trade at posts along the river, they caught the disease and carried it back with them into Rupert's Land. Once again, just as in 1781, contagion swept the prairie. One witness described "lodges standing on every hill, but not a streak of smoke rising from them. Not a sound can be heard to break the awful stillness, save the ominous croak of the ravens, and mournful howl of wolves fattening on the human carcasses that lie strewed around. It seems as if the very genius of desolation had stalked through the prairies, and wreaked his vengeance on everything bearing the shape of humanity." By late fall the disease had reached the banks of the North Saskatchewan where it petered out in the face of a vaccination campaign mounted by the Hudson's Bay Company. The result was that the Cree people were spared excessive loss. The other Plains groups were not so lucky. Two-thirds of the Assiniboine people are believed to have died in the epidemic, and traders estimated that three-quarters of all the Plains people were wiped out.

More gradual than smallpox, but every bit as fatal, was the annihilation of the buffalo. In the early years of the century, the prairie was black with migrating herds of these animals, and in the spring it was common to find the river banks littered with the rotting carcasses of bison which had been caught crossing the ice at breakup and thus were swept away on the rampaging current. Alexander Henry reported seeing a continuous line of drowned animals borne on the current for two days and two nights past his post on the Red River in 1801. However, by mid-century over-hunting for hides and robes, as well as meat, was drastically reducing the herds and driving them further to the south and west. As buffalo sought refuge in the shadow of the Rockies, Indians fought over the few remaining hunting grounds until finally there were no animals left and the proud Plains people were reduced to eating their horses and begging for help. Like their Woodland neighbours before them, they fell into a state of economic reliance on the strangers in their land.

As the Indians coped with change as best they could, the Hudson's Bay Company was enjoying a period of sustained prosperity. Austerity was good business; fur returns remained healthy and so did profits. In the middle years of the century the Company recorded average annual earnings of £60,000 and Rupert's Land still produced well over fifty thousand beaver pelts a year, as well as large amounts of "small furs." Most of these furs came from the distant northern districts; southern areas were valued principally as buffer zones to deflect American competition or as sources of food for the northern brigades. The logistics of supplying the deep North and transporting its furs to markets were formidable. The entire interchange took as long as five years between the time trade goods were ordered from a tiny post on the Mackenzie River and the actual sale of furs traded for those goods at auction in London. If a boat upset, a *voyageur* deserted, a ship foundered or any one of countless other accidents intervened, the whole process could be stalled for yet another season, at great cost to the Company.

It was Governor Simpson's great accomplishment to recognize that time and space were the Company's worst enemies and to work out an efficient and economical system of overcoming them. The most prominent feature of this system was the York boat, "that cumbrous old failure of a sailboat." Modelled on the sharpended Orkney fish boat, with shallow draught to navigate inland waterways, the York boat was, like so much else in the fur trade, a blend of old world and new. Boats were used sparingly around 1780, but in the period after union they came into their own, replacing canoes on all the major transport routes. About twelve metres in length and rowed by as many as eight oarsmen, a York boat could handle three and a half tons of cargo, was more seaworthy than the light bark canoe, and much more durable.

Less glamour has collected around the native "tripmen" who muscled the York boats across the West than around the French *voyageurs* in their graceful canoes. True, there was little enough glamour in the work. Not only were there larger cargoes to pack across the portages but the unwieldy boats themselves had to be rolled over log roads or hauled across by block and tackle. And then, of course, there was hour after hour of pulling on the leaden oars. "The work is so laborious that some Kill themselves by it," wrote one veteran, "and many are sprung and so disabled that it makes old men of them before they come to the prime of life." The work was unpopular enough that it was left to mixed-blood and Indian casuals. Each June the brigade departed the Red River colony, more than a dozen boats in all, laden with pemmican and other food supplies. After crossing Lake Winnipeg it put in at Norway House to take on trade goods carried up from York Factory. Then it was up the familiar route via Cumberland House to the Methye Portage at the height of land. This well-worn portage was too long to be crossed by the heavy boats, and goods carried across it were handed over to another brigade waiting at the northern end to complete the journey to Athabasca and beyond. The Red River men, their boats now heavy with fur packs, turned back toward Norway House, where they dropped cargo, then home to the colony after an absence of four months. Such was the summer routine until steamboats began to ply the western waterways later in the century.

In the winter, life at the posts went on much as it had for generations, the boring routine broken only by the arrival of the mail sled or the celebration of a public holiday. "The chief drawback to letter writing at a remote post," complained one Company man, "is the total absence of any thing to write about." Over the years fur trade society had become highly stratified. The ranks of the Company were divided into two groups — officers, or gentlemen, and ordinary servants — and few men crossed the broad gulf which lay between. The servant class was a mixed bag, ranging from labourers who did most of the common chores about the post to skilled tradesmen, coopers, blacksmiths, masons, and carpenters, who manufactured trade goods and boats and kept the posts in good repair. Since the trade was conducted in several languages — English, French, Gaelic and a profusion of native tongues — interpreters were particularly valuable members of this class. At the other end of the social scale were the "commissioned gentlemen," the governor, his chief factors and traders, and the clerks from whom they were recruited. These men were the gentry of the trade and liked to keep their distance from the ordinary servants. They ate at separate tables, received such delicacies as brandy, butter, and preserved fruits, and bought goods at the Company store for reduced prices. The most puffed-up even required servants to doff caps in their presence. Of the officer class, the most privileged were the chief factors. These "aristocrats" were attended by valets and cooks; they dined with monogrammed silver and drank from the best crystal; they had their daughters tutored in singing and piano and packed them off to school in the outside world as soon as they were of age. "This exalted functionary was lord paramount," one observer recalled, his word was law; he was necessarily surrounded by a halo of dignity, and his person was sacred, so to speak. He was dressed in a suit of black or dark blue, white shirt, collars to the ears, frock coat, velvet stock and straps to the bottom of his trousers. When he went out of doors he wore a black beaver hat worth forty shillings. When travelling in a canoe or boat, he was lifted in and out of the craft by the crew. . . . In camp his tent was pitched apart from the shelter given his crew. He had a separate fire, and the first work of the boat's crew after landing was to pitch his tent, clear his camp, and collect firewood sufficient for the night before they were allowed to attend to their own wants. Salutes were fired on his departure from the fort and his return All this ceremony was considered necessary; it had a good effect on the Indians; it added to his dignity in the eyes of his subordinates. . . .

The chief factor had come a long way from his grizzled counterpart, the pedlar, huddled in his log hut on the banks of the Saskatchewan, and there were some veterans who did not think the change was for the better. "How pitiful these cake and basket excursions must appear to such men as Sir A. Mc. [Alexander Mackenzie] and Wm. McGillivray who used to walk their 6 and 700 mile on snow shoes for the pleasure of taking a Christmas dinner with a friend," Colin Robertson wrote in disgust, "not like our modern *voyageurs* who are drove from post to post in a dog cariol, like a packet of letters and enveloped much in the same manner. . . ." Almost without exception these Company officers were Europeans; "a parcel of upstart Scotch men" as one disgruntled source called them. Mixed-bloods filled the common ranks but were not trusted with access to the upper echelons of power and influence. It was a society shot through with snobbery and bigotry, often affecting an awkward and ludicrous gentility and lacking the informality and equality of former times.

One of the key events in the transformation of fur trade society was the arrival of white women in the fur country. The company had always opposed the presence of European wives at its posts, thinking them a useless expense, taking up space and supplies without contributing any labour in return. It was customary for men to take native wives and even to have "double families" — one in the Northwest and another waiting at home. However, following union, several European women immigrated to the colony at Red River and in 1830 Governor Simpson brought his own bride, Frances, to live in the fur country. Simpson passed on his own racism to his wife. He discouraged her from having anything to do with mixed-blood women in the settlement and thereby put an official stamp of approval on a growing tendency to view native women in an inferior light. Simpson himself had always treated his "bits of brown" as mistresses, not wives, and this personal prejudice was turning into social convention, strengthened by the attitude of missionaries who were coming into the country preaching against the sins of country marriages. Many Company officers followed their Governor's example by importing European wives and what had once been a fairly integrated society was now divided by racial animosity. It became unthinkable to marry an Indian woman and mixed-blood wives were valued less for their fur trade skills than for their level of acculturation. "Nothing can give greater comfort to a husband than the satisfaction of having a wife who is nearly mute," wrote Chief Factor Donald Mackenzie, reflecting the new idea that a good wife was devout, meek, and talented along domestic lines rather than a useful partner in the business of trade. "Indian wives were at one time the vogue," recalled James Douglas in 1840, "the half breed supplanted these, and now we have the lovely tender exotic torn from its parent bed, to pine and languish in the desert." Just as natives were losing some of their bargaining power in the fur trade economy, so their status in fur trade society was deteriorating as the standards of Victorian England insinuated themselves into the Northwest.

An incident occurred in Red River in 1850 which showed how the values of European society were carried into the fur country, cloaked in snobbish provincialism. Sarah Ballenden was the mixed-blood wife of the Company's chief officer at the settlement. As such she was the leading hostess in the colony, carrying out her social duties with enough grace and energy to earn the jealousy of many of the European women who did not like being overshadowed by a "half-breed." Rumours about Mrs. Ballenden's moral character circulated through the settlement, especially about her relationship with a retired army officer, Christopher Foss. Though there was no hard evidence to suggest anything but innocent friendship between Foss and the chief trader's wife, this did not stop the gossips and Mrs. Ballenden found herself snubbed by polite, that is, white society. Eventually whispered innuendo became public scandalmongering when a Company clerk named Pelly repeated the charges against Foss and Ballenden to Governor Simpson. Foss immediately sued for defamation on behalf of Mrs. Ballenden, and that summer a jury found in her favour. The colony was split into two camps over the scandal; on the one side clergy and Company officers who wanted native women, and by implication all native people, kept in their place; on the other, the settlement's mixed-bloods and their non-native spouses. It was, in the phrase of one witness, "a strife of blood." Nor did the court case settle matters. For a few months the Ballendens lived quietly out of the public eye but that winter the chief factor went to Britain about his health and before too long his wife was once again the object of rumour and scandal involving her relationship with Captain Foss. Her husband stood by her after his return but he was soon posted to the West Coast and Sarah went to live at Norway House, an outcast and an emblem of the sour bigotry which was poisoning fur trade society.

Meanwhile the trade itself entered its final decades, at least its final decades as the pre-eminent activity in the Canadian West. They were not tranquil years for the Hudson's Bay Company, even though profits were good. European fur markets were unstable and by the 1840s silk hats were replacing beaver on the heads of the most fashionable.

More troublesome was the challenge to the Company's monopoly in Rupert's Land posed by the growth of illicit trade in and around Red River. Free trade was an understandable response to the limited possibilities in the tiny colony. A very small market existed for farm produce. The celebrated buffalo hunt occupied the mixed-blood people for several weeks and afterwards they could sign on as tripmen with the Company's brigades; but after that, what? No monopoly rights granted by some foreign monarch across the ocean could be expected to deter the Red River population from picking up extra money by doing a little trading for furs themselves. And actually the Company did not much mind competition on such a small scale. Furs wound up in its stores anyway since there was no one else to whom the free traders could sell them. Then, in 1844, this easy tolerance was shaken with the arrival of an American trader at Pembina just south of the border. Now free traders had an alternative market to the Hudson's Bay Company. Company officials retaliated by restricting the importation of trade goods and otherwise regulating commerce in the colony. But free traders were resourceful at avoiding the watchful eye of the Company and without a police force there was not really much it could do to halt the flow of furs southward. For a couple of years Simpson was able to get some British troops garrisoned in the colony, ostensibly to defend against American invasion but actually to defend the Company against its own settlers. But the soldiers were withdrawn and free trade flourished.

Matters came to a head in 1849. The Company's chief factor, John Ballenden, decided to try to stop the free traders through the courts. Early in the year he brought charges against a party of four Métis for illegally trafficking in furs. The case came to trial on May 17, heard before the colony's chief judicial officer, Adam Thom, a man much hated by the Métis for his notorious anti-French sympathies. The French-speaking mixed-bloods were greatly aroused by the trial. For them it was much more than a simple case of whether four of their fellows had broken the laws of the colony. The Métis by this time saw themselves as a "new nation," a people apart, a group with political and economic claims arising from their historic connection with the country. This new nationalism, forged in the buffalo country and on the brigades, would one day soon lead the Métis into open rebellion. In May 1849, they were demanding the legal right to trade anywhere, with anyone. They gathered outside the court, listening to speeches by Louis Riel, father of the rebel leader, brandishing their guns in the air and threatening to over-run the trial.

The first of the accused supposed to appear was Guillaume Sayer; instead, a delegation of mixed-bloods led by the prominent free trader James Sinclair presented itself before the court. It was agreed that Sayer would come forward and that Sinclair would be his counsel. While the excited mob milled restlessly outside, evidence was heard and a jury composed in part of Métis found Sayer guilty "of Trading Furs." Ballenden was elated; the verdict seemed to vindicate the Company's claim to its monopoly. He did not object when the court recognized the jury's plea for mercy by letting Sayer off without punishment; nor when charges against the other free traders were dropped. However, when the doors of the courtroom swung open and the crowd outside learned the outcome — Sayer was free to go without penalty — a wholly different interpretation was put on matters. "*La Commerce est libre,*" the people shouted, shooting off their guns in wild celebration. "The Trade is free." And so it was. Never again did the Company bother to defend its right to exclusive trade in the courts. Instead it chose to compete using tactics which had been successful for close to two hundred years; it chose to underbid and outsell the free traders, rather than intimidate them. In this way the Company managed to keep control of the western trade.

In the decades following 1821 the fur trade was synonymous with the Hudson's Bay Company. To discuss one was to discuss the other. Free traders abounded, and some of them flourished, but they did not challenge the Company's position as main employer, social arbiter, and virtual government in the Northwest. By 1857 the Company employed three thousand men, not including the Indian trappers who actually collected the furs or the native hunters who supplied so much of the food. It was the sole market for the produce grown in the Northwest and the sole promoter of industrial or manufacturing schemes. In most places its posts were hospital, grocery store, post office, and church to the population. Yet, for all the Company's power and profits, new forces were at work in the Northwest which threatened its hegemony. In 1859 steamboats began to ply north from the United States and soon they were a common sight on western waterways. York boats were mothballed and brigades disbanded as the economics of transportation made it cheaper to import goods by rail and steamboat from the United States than through the venerable depot at York Factory. After two hundred years the Hudson Bay route to the interior fell into disuse. Meanwhile, in Canada and in Great Britain influential voices were raised against the Company as an outdated example of monopoly in an era of free trade. It was portrayed as a feudal despotism, demoralizing Indians and European settlers alike. Most importantly, businessmen and promoters in eastern Canada were awakening to the possibilities of the Northwest. With visionary zeal, they talked of spanning the territory with railways and telegraph lines and filling the "empty" spaces with industrious agriculturalists. As assimilation of the West began to gain popularity in eastern Canada, the Hudson's Bay Company recognized that the days of the fur trade frontier were numbered, that the new forces could not be denied. Instead of making trouble, therefore, the Company decided to make a deal.

CHAPTER NINE

Speculators in Civilization

In September 1860, George Simpson died at his house in Lachine. For forty years the fur trade had been his preoccupation; for thirty-four years, ever since the Hudson's Bay Company made him its Overseas Governor, he had been the most powerful individual in the Canadian Northwest. Under his direction the trade enjoyed several decades of unbroken profitability and he was knighted for his services to the Crown. And yet, in the later years of his career, Simpson was distancing himself from the trade. He and his wife had gone to live at Red River in 1830 but found fur trade society impossibly vulgar, so they took up residence in a house the Company built for them at Lachine just outside Montreal. Of course, the governor continued to make regular visits to the Northwest to oversee the trade but more and more he involved himself in the business life of eastern Canada. Investing his income in a variety of projects, he began to amass a respectable fortune and a degree of political influence. Simpson's interests included railways, canals, mines, and banks, projects which by their nature involved him in lobbying with public officials. From his experience in the fur trade he knew well how to grease the wheels of commerce with gifts. Enjoying his exotic connection with the western frontier, Simpson would soften the appropriate politician with "presents" of buffalo tongues and canoes, and more sizeable bribes when the stakes were high. Nor were his dealings limited to the lower ranks; in an attempt to win government contracts for a shipping line in which he was involved, Simpson offered bribes to the Prime Minister himself. Unfortunately, the government fell before his "seed money" yielded results. The governor usually enjoyed better luck, however, and at his death he was worth more than £100,000.

Simpson's involvement in the commercial life of eastern Canada was symbolic of a growing interpenetration of East and West which was leading to a breakdown in the isolation of the fur country. During his years as governor, the trade prospered, yet it was becoming at the same time evident that the Northwest was not going to remain the private preserve of the Hudson's Bay Company for very much longer. As the century reached its mid-point a noisy collection of free traders, promoters, and entre-preneurs was pressing at the frontiers of the Company's domain, wanting to get in. And it was not the fur trade which attracted them.

Since 1821 the Hudson's Bay Company had enjoyed its trade monopoly in relative obscurity. Aside from a handful of free traders, no one else was interested in the western frontier; indeed it was assumed by most people to be a frozen wasteland populated by ferocious natives. However, at mid-century events conspired to bring the Hudson's Bay Company and its regime into the harsh light of publicity.

First of all, a coalition of free traders and disgruntled former employees opposed to Company rule in the West approached the British government with its complaints. It had to be admitted that the Company was something of a dinosaur left over from a previous age when monopolies sanctioned by the Crown were still popular. In the nineteenth century the chartered monopoly was no longer favoured by most politicians and the anti-monopoly faction received a fair opportunity to paint its lurid picture of an unprincipled business concern making unconscionable profits by debauching the Indians and holding half a continent in thrall. By themselves this group of critics could not convince the Colonial Office to take action but during the 1850s their complaints were taken up and embellished in eastern Canada by a disparate group of entrepreneurs, journalists, and speculators. The Canadian colonies were suffering a severe bout of railway fever. As part of this enthusiasm, rail promoters resurrected the age-old plan to reach across the continent to the Western Sea, this time with a ribbon of iron. Apparently the dream of connecting Europe and the Orient via America would not die. Of course, this time around railway promoters could strengthen their case by pointing out the importance of assimilating the top half of the continent into the British Empire before the Americans grabbed it. At the same time Ontario was flexing its muscle. A growing population was running out of land to settle and cultivate, and in Toronto an ambitious merchant class longed to make Rupert's Land its economic hinterland. All of these various visions and interests were knit together into a vigorous expansionist movement which campaigned to annex the Northwest to Canada. Indeed, some even argued that Canada already owned Rupert's Land as an inheritance from the French, and the Hudson's Bay Company was a squatter which should be evicted with haste. The Colonial Office was not about to act so precipitately; however, a special committee was convened to investigate conditions in the Northwest. This committee found much of the suspicion and criticism of Company rule overblown, but, nevertheless, the writing was on the wall for those who cared to read it. The fur trade would have to accommodate itself to the forces of change.

The Hudson's Bay Company was not necessarily opposed to surrendering its privileged position. The Company had lost its monopoly trading license in 1859 anyway, and it was prepared to abandon its chartered rights to Rupert's Land. Experience was swiftly proving that Company traders could hold their own in a free market without the protection of the monopoly. The colony at Red River was a burden to look after and land-hungry settlers would soon be coming into the territory. "As the country comes to be occupied without our leave," predicted the Overseas Governor, Alexander Dallas, "they will bye and bye not even give us thanks." Why not make the best of it by getting healthy compensation for chartered rights that weren't worth much anyway? "In another year our privileges will be worth little or nothing," admitted Dallas in 1862, "and any compensation we may receive, will be so much clear gain. . . ." But not everyone in the Company was as anxious as Dallas to sell out. In London, Governor Henry Hulse Berens played his hand closer to the vest. He was prepared to sell the charter, but at his own price. Assuring the other players in the game that he did not want "to impede the speculators in civilization if we are fairly treated," he set the stakes at £1,500,000 and sat back to see who would stay and who would fold. The Colonial Office folded; it could see no way that the undeveloped resources of Rupert's Land could justify such an expenditure. Canada followed suit; even if it could raise the money it was not politically mature enough to annex such an unwieldy territory. That left private capital the only bidder still in the game, in the person of Edward Watkin.

Edward Watkin was a fixer. A railway manager of broad experience in Great Britain, he was sent to Canada in 1861 by the financial backers of the beleagured Grand Trunk Railway. This line, intended to be the commercial backbone of British North America, was mired in financial difficulties. Friendly politicians had bailed it out before with funds but there was a limit to how long the ailing line could feed at the public trough. Watkin's solution, like his character, was audacious, even impertinent. Instead of pulling in his horns, he decided that the answer to the Grand Trunk's difficulties was expansion across the continent to the Pacific. Watkin was a proponent of the Imperial idea; he envisioned the day when all of British America would be united like a ribbon of red running from sea to sea. And, conveniently, his railway would tie the cumbersome territory together.

An ambitious project like a trans-continental railway took time to mature, involving as it did the support of politicians as well as financiers. Meanwhile, Watkin embarked on a scheme to build a telegraph line across the Northwest as a precursor to the rail line. But whether the line was wire or iron, Watkin came up against what he called "the heavy weight and obstruction of the Hudson's Bay Company." When he approached the Company about ceding a substantial corridor of land through its chartered territory, Governor Berens made it quite clear that his co-operation would be limited to a narrow strip just wide enough to run the telegraph. He was suspicious that Watkin and his associates wanted a generous grant of land in order to sell some of it to underwrite their project, and, as far as Berens was concerned, if anyone wanted the Company's land, they would have to pay his price for it. "If these gentlemen are so patriotic," he grumbled sarcastically, "why don't they buy us out?" As it turned out, Watkin was impatient and confident enough to do just that. During the winter of 1862-63 he and his group sat down with Berens and eventually agreed to meet his price, even though Watkin had no idea when the deal was made where he was going to find the money. Berens wanted cash and the British government had already made it clear they would not get involved so Watkin turned at the last moment to the International Financial Society. This association of merchant bankers had been formed only a month before to provide risk capital for ventures around the world. During its years of operation the Society's investments would include railways in eastern Europe, a land company in Mauritius, and banks in Italy, but in June 1863, it put up the money to buy the Hudson's Bay Company. Technically, it was the stock, not the Company itself, which was sold. The International Financial Society bought Company shares at a price three times their market value, then reissued new stock which, when sold, brought the Society a tidy profit of £300,000. Sir Edmund Head, former Governor-General of Canada, was installed as Governor of the Company and a new board of directors was appointed. These men took over the direction of affairs and the Financial Society, having served its purpose and reaped its reward, dropped from view. As for Watkin, the chief architect of the changeover, he now expected to have no trouble launching his telegraph. Hurrying to Canada as an agent of the Company he sent a surveyor into the field and began to amass supplies. But he had not reckoned with the speed with which the new leaders of the Hudson's Bay Company would come to see things from a fresh perspective. From the outside the Company had seemed a mere impediment to progress. Now that they were involved in its management, however, the telegraph did not appear so urgent to the directors. Watkin was chastised for moving ahead so quickly and called home for consultation. Impatient as always, and angry at this apparent betrayal of his plans, Watkin went off in a huff and the telegraph was not built.

For the fur trade, the significance of the sale of the Hudson's Bay Company in 1863 lay in the plans of its new directors. A prospectus issued by the Company promised land sales, colonization projects, and communication links, and it was obvious that land, not furs, had become the most attractive resource in the Northwest. Typical of the new attitude abroad in the Company was the fact that the "wintering traders" in the Northwest had no inkling at all that a sale was in the offing until after it took place. Chief factors and traders saw themselves almost as partners in the Company but here they were being treated like common employees, "sold like dumb driven cattle" as one of them complained. What better indication was there that the fur trade, and the men who prosecuted it, were no longer the principal concern of the "Honourable Company"? The new owners were speculators in future settlement, not present trade. Fifty years before, the fur trade dictated events in the Northwest. By the 1860s a new era was dawning, one in which trade was just one of many activities and certainly not the most important. As the Northwest prepared to welcome a flood of settlement which would transform it into a vast agricultural frontier, the fur trade was fading into the background.

In many ways there is a discontinuity between the fur trade years in the Northwest and events which followed, almost as if time had jumped its rails and gone careening off in a new direction. Buffalo herds disappeared, waterways fell silent, the Indians were pushed onto their reservations and the old forts mouldered and collapsed. Railways were built across the West, shifting the focus of settlement away from the riverbanks to the ribbon of track. Homesteaders replaced fur traders on the far frontier. Quite suddenly, agriculture became the most important activity and the West was being hailed as a new "granary of the world." It seemed a complete break with the past.

The eclipse of the fur trade was no great tragedy for Canada. Furs had not been exported via the old St. Lawrence route since 1821 and it was back before the turn of the century since the trade had made a significant contribution to the wealth of the colonies. Aside from French-Canadian canoemen labouring in the West, it was the British who profited from the trade. Its main contribution to Canada was that traders conveniently occupied the Northwest until the colonies were strong enough to reach out and assimilate it. Then, of course, once the Northwest became part of Canada, the fur trade became part of Canada's history.

Yet the trade did not pass away without leaving its mark. Like any series of events in the past, it has a legacy, something it handed on to the people who came after. For one thing, the trade determined the rough contours of the territory which would become the nation of Canada. When Harold Innis claimed that "Canada emerged as a political entity with boundaries largely determined by the fur trade" he was understating the influence of other, equally important factors. To take just one example, if the trade truly determined borders then northern Washington state would belong to Canada. Nevertheless, the Innis insight was a valid one. If exact boundaries are not always traceable to the fur trade, it did set the precedent for an east-west orientation to the continent. By crossing the plains and climbing the Rockies, traders showed that it was possible to establish an east-west flow of goods and information which could link such a sprawling piece of real estate into a coherent whole. The fur traders showed that trans-continental unity was possible. Whether it was likely, necessary, or even beneficial was a matter for future generations to decide.

For the native people; Indians and Métis; the legacy of the fur trade was a mixed one. The Métis, of course, would not exist had the trade not brought together Frenchman and Indian in the first place. Nor would they perhaps exist as a culturally distinct, politically conscious group if the trade had not given them a chance to establish a unique place for themselves in the West. Actually, for both Indian and Métis, the trade was much less exploitative than it might have been. One only has to look at the experience of other European nations in America, notably the Spanish in Latin America, to recognize that the fur trade was a relatively humane enterprise. This is not because of any innate moral superiority of the traders; it is simply because they relied on the natives for food and furs and had no reason to interfere with their traditional way of life in order to obtain what they wanted. Native people eagerly adopted metal goods and weapons into their cultures but this did not mean they were slaves to the European traders or did not have a shrewd capacity to manipulate the relationship to their advantage. However, along with the trade came alcohol and disease and in its wake came immigration and settlement. Populations were decimated, food supplies were wiped out and land was expropriated. Reeling from these blows, the Indian and Métis people could not defend themselves. Their land was occupied and they became outsiders in their own country. The struggle being waged by native people today for equality and dignity in Canadian society has its roots in this period of our history.

In an economic sense, the fur trade did not so much affect subsequent developments as set a precedent which they followed. The trade was a classic example of foreign ownership and exploitation of Canadian natural resources, a phenomenon which is all too familiar today. The Hudson's Bay Company was the prototype of the foreign multi-national, extracting wealth from Canada and exporting it back to the metropolis. From the very beginning the Canadian economy was dependent on foreign markets and foreign capital, established as a resource-producing hinterland for a foreign metropolis. It is ironic that past historians have been so quick to point out, rather too smugly, how native people surrendered their independence to foreign traders in return for certain improvements in their standard of living. Dependence has, in fact, long been the central feature of the Canadian economy; the fur trade was just the first example of it. In this sense, all Canadians are "Indians in the fur trade" and the fur trade is the story of all Canadians.

Sources Consulted

General

This study is based on the many journals, letters, memoirs, diaries, and trading post records which have been published over the years. They will be found below, listed according to the relevant chapters. In this regard, every fur trade researcher is indebted to the Hudson's Bay Company which has made so many of its valuable records available in published form under the imprint of the Hudson's Bay Record Society. Other, more general, secondary sources provided both information and theoretical insights. Harold Innis, *The Fur Trade in Canada* (revised edition, Toronto: University of Toronto Press, 1956) is a treasure trove of fact and synthesis which remains a classic in its field despite recent misgivings (see, for example, W. J. Eccles, "A Belated Review of Harold Adams Innis, *The Fur Trade in Canada*," *Canadian Historical Review,* LX, 1979; 419-441). More readable in style but even lengthier than Innis is Arthur S. Morton, *A History of the Canadian West to 1870-71* (second edition, Toronto: University of Toronto Press, 1973). A more concise narrative is provided by the British fur trade historian, E. E. Rich, *The Fur Trade and the Northwest to 1857* (Toronto: McClelland and Stewart, 1967). Rich's masterwork is *The Hudson's Bay Company, 1670-1870* (Toronto: McClelland and Stewart, 3 vols., 1960). Several excellent recent studies have focussed on particular aspects of the fur trade. The economics of the trade and its impact on native people is the subject of two books by Arthur J. Ray, *Indians in the Fur Trade*

(Toronto: University of Toronto Press, 1974) and, with Donald Freeman, *"Give Us Good Measure": An Economic Analysis of Relations Between the Indians and the Hudson's Bay Company before 1763* (Toronto: University of Toronto Press, 1978). Family life and the role of women are dealt with in Sylvia Van Kirk, *"Many Tender Ties": Women in Fur Trade Society, 1670-1870* (Winnipeg: Watson and Dwyer, 1980) and Jennifer Brown, *"Strangers in Blood": Fur Trade Company Families in Indian Country* (Vancouver: University of British Columbia Press, 1980). Finally, a handy introduction to the most recent fur trade research is the collection of essays edited by Arthur Ray and Carol Judd, *Old Trails and New Directions: Papers of the Third North American Fur Trade Conference* (Toronto: University of Toronto Press, 1980).

Chapter One: The French in the West

The story of La Vérendrye's exploits is found in L. J. Burpee, ed., *Journals and Letters of Pierre Gaultier de Varennes de La Vérendrye and his Sons* (Toronto: The Champlain Society, 1927). Burpee also edited Anthony Henday's journal, "York Factory to the Blackfeet Country, the Journal of Anthony Henday, 1754-55," *Proceedings and Transactions of the Royal Society of Canada* (Third Series, Vol. 1, 1907: 307-364). Less useful but still interesting is the journal of Jacques Repentigny Legardeur de Saint-Pierre, *Report on Canadian Archives* (Ottawa: 1886). For the material on the Hudson's Bay Company see E. E. Rich's history of the Company and K. G. Davies, ed., *Letters from Hudson Bay, 1703-40* (London: Hudson's Bay Record Society, 1965).

Chapter Two: Pedlars from Quebec

The pedlars did not leave many accounts of themselves. One who did was Alexander Henry, *Travels and Adventures in Canada and the Indian Territories Between the Years 1760 and 1776* (Reprinted edition, Edmonton: M. G. Hurtig, 1969). Harold Innis quotes liberally from Peter Pond's autobiography in *Peter Pond: Fur Trader and Adventurer* (Toronto: Irwin and Gordon, 1930) and there is a good deal of material relating to the pedlars in W. S. Wallace, ed., *Documents Relating to the North West Company* (Toronto: The Champlain Society, 1934). Two collections of documents which cover the Hudson's Bay Company penetration of the interior are J. B. Tyrrell, ed., *Journal of Samuel Hearne and Philip Turnor* (Toronto: The Champlain Society, 1934) and E. E. Rich, ed., *Cumberland House Journals and Inland Journals, 1775-1782* (London: Hudson's Bay Record Society, 2 vols., 1951-52). See also an important article by Richard Glover, "The Difficulties of the Hudson's Bay Company's Penetration of the West," *Canadian Historical Review,* XXIX, 1948: pp. 240-254.

Chapter Three: Traders and Indians

The details of life and trade in the Northwest can be gathered from a variety of published accounts. The Hudson's Bay Company perspective is available in Glyndwr Williams ed., *Andrew Graham's Observations on Hudson's Bay, 1767-1791* (London: Hudson's Bay Record Society, 1969) and Alice M. Johnson, ed., *Saskatchewan Journals and Correspondence* (London: Hudson's Bay Record Society, 1967). Nor'wester accounts are found in Elliott Coues, ed., *New Light on the Early History of the Greater Northwest: The Manuscript Journals of Alexander Henry and David Thompson* (Minneapolis: Ross and Haines, 2 vols., 1897); Charles M. Gates, ed., *Five Fur Traders of the Northwest* (St. Paul, Minn.: Minnesota Historical Society, 1965); Daniel Williams Harmon, *Sixteen Years in the Indian Country* (Toronto: Macmillan, 1957); L. R. Masson, ed., *Les Bourgeois de la Compagnie du Nord-Ouest* (New York: Antiquarian Press, 2 vols., 1960); and A. S. Morton, ed., *Journal of Duncan McGillivray* (Toronto: Macmillan, 1929). An excellent study of the Indian perspective is John Milloy, *The Plains Cree: A Preliminary Trade and Military Chronology, 1670-1870* (Ottawa: Unpublished Master's Thesis, Carleton University, 1972).

Chapter Four: Two Caesars

The career of Alexander Mackenzie is covered in W. Kaye Lamb, ed., *The Journals and Letters of Sir Alexander Mackenzie* (Cambridge: Cambridge University Press, 1970). W. S. Wallace, *The Pedlars from Quebec* (Toronto: Ryerson Press, 1954) has much relevant information about the protagonists, as does Elaine Allan Mitchell, "New Evidence on the Mackenzie-McTavish Break," *Canadian Historical Review* XLI, 1960: pp. 41-47. High life in Montreal is described by Colonel G. T. Landmann, *Adventures and Recollections* (London: Colburn and Co., 1852). An admittedly biased account of Canadian trading practises is Thomas Douglas Selkirk, *A Sketch of the British Fur Trade in North America* (London: James Ridgway, 1816). The best description of the XY Company remains an unpublished doctoral thesis by R. A. Pendergast, *The XY Company: 1798-1804* (University of Ottawa, 1957).

Chapter Five: Race Across the Rockies

Two editions of David Thompson's autobiographical writings have been published, both with introductions: Richard Glover, ed., *David Thompson's Narrative, 1784-1812* (Toronto: The Champlain Society, 1962) and Victor Hopwood, ed., *David Thompson: Travels in Western North America, 1784-1812* (Toronto: Macmillan, 1971). Simon Fraser's expedition is described in W. Kaye Lamb, ed., *The Letters and Journals of Simon Fraser, 1806-1808* (Toronto: Macmillan, 1960). For the American fur trade see Paul Phillips, *The Fur Trade* (Norman, Okla.: University of Oklahoma Press, 2 vols., 1961) and David Lavender, *A Fist in the Wilderness* (New York: Doubleday, 1964).

Chapter Six: The Battle for Athabasca

The best biography of Lord Selkirk remains John Morgan Gray, *Lord Selkirk of Red River* (Toronto: Macmillan, 1964). The career of his chief antagonist is described in Marjorie Wilkins Campbell,

Northeast to the Sea: A Biography of William McGillivray (Toronto: Clarke, Irwin, 1975). An excellent book on the Métis position is Margaret Macleod and W. L. Morton, *Cuthbert Grant of Grantown* (Toronto: McClelland and Stewart, 1963). Events in Athabasca are described in two volumes edited by E. E. Rich, *Journal of Occurrences in the Athabasca Department by George Simpson, 1820 and 1821* (London: Hudson's Bay Record Society, 1938) and *Colin Robertson's Correspondence Book, 1817-1822* (London: Hudson's Bay Record Society, 1939). An instructive article by K. G. Davies, "From Competition to Union," in *Aspects of the Fur Trade: Selected Papers of the 1965 North American Fur Trade Conference* (St. Paul, Minn.: Minnesota Historical Society, 1967) relates the various attempts at merging the two companies prior to 1821.

Chapter Seven: Losing the Oregon Territory

The reorganization of the Hudson's Bay Company, following union, is covered in R. Harvey Fleming, ed., *Minutes of Council, Northern Department of Rupert Land, 1821-1831* (London: Hudson's Bay Record Society, 1940). John McLoughlin's correspondence has been collected in three volumes edited by E. E. Rich, *The Letters of John McLoughlin, 1825-1846* (London: Hudson's Bay Record Society, 1941-44). George Simpson's visits to the West Coast are the subject of two volumes: Frederick Merk, ed., *Fur Trade and Empire* (Cambridge, Mass.: Harvard University Press, 1968) and E. E. Rich, ed., *Simpson's 1828 Journey to the Columbia* (London: Hudson's Bay Record Society, 1947). For Ogden and the Snake River expeditions, see E. E. Rich, ed., *Ogden's Snake Country Journals, 1824-26* (London: Hudson's Bay Record Society, 1950), K. G. Davies, ed., *Peter Skene Ogden's Snake Country Journal, 1826-27* (London: Hudson's Bay Record Society, 1961) and Glyndwr Williams, ed., *Peter Skene Ogden's Snake Country Journals, 1827-29* (London: Hudson's Bay Record Society, 1971). The "Oregon Question" is dealt with exhaustively in Frederick Merk, *The Oregon Question* (Cambridge, Mass.: Harvard University Press, 1967) and also in John S. Galbraith, *The Hudson's Bay Company as an Imperial Factor, 1821-1869* (Los Angeles: University of California Press, 1957). Two biographers of George Simpson are A. S. Morton, *Sir George Simpson* (Toronto: J. M. Dent, 1944) and John S. Galbraith, *The Little Emperor: Governor Simpson of the Hudson's Bay Company* (Toronto: Macmillan, 1976).

Chapter Eight: The New Regime: "A Strife of Blood"

The colony of Red River is described in E. E. Rich, ed., *London Correspondence Inward from Eden Colville, 1849-1852* (London: Hudson's Bay Record Society, 1956). A female perspective on life in the Northwest is Margaret Arnett Macleod, ed., *The Letters of Letitia Hargrave* (Toronto: The Champlain Society, 1947). The Hudson's Bay Company labour force is described exhaustively in Philip Goldring, *Papers on the Labour System of the Hudson's Bay Company, 1821-1900* (Ottawa: Parks Canada, 2 vols., 1979-80). The best account of the York boat is Richard Glover's "York Boats," *The Beaver*, March 1949. A classic work on the Métis is Marcel Giraud, *Le Métis canadien* (Paris: Université de Paris, 1945). For women, and social life generally, see the works by Sylvia Van Kirk and Jennifer Brown cited earlier.

Chapter Nine: Speculators in Civilization

The sale of the Hudson's Bay Company in 1863 is covered in Galbraith's history of the Company. For Edward Watkin, see his memoir, *Canada and the States: Recollections, 1851-1886* (London: Ward, Lock and Co., 1887), as well as two articles, Elaine Allen Mitchell, "Edward Watkin and the Buying Out of the Hudson's Bay Company," *Canadian Historical Review*, XXXIV, 1953: pp. 219-244; and Andrew Robb, "Edward Watkin and the Pacific Telegraph, 1861-1865," *Ontario History*, LXV, 1973: pp. 189-209. The expansionist movement in Canada is treated in Douglas Owram, *Promise of Eden: The Canadian Expansionist Movement and the Idea of the West, 1856-1900* (Toronto: University of Toronto Press, 1980).

Index

River, 117, 119-23;
competition with Americans,
91; competition with Hudson's
Bay Company 7, 66-67,
113-14, 125-28, 145;
competition with Montreal
traders, 46-47, 76-77;
competition with XY
Company, 78-81; in the
Columbia district, 141, 142;
labour force, 51-52, 61-62;
merger with Hudson's Bay
Company, 128-32;
organization, 51-53, 69, 85,
131; origins, 45-46, 74
Norway House, 163

O

Ochagach, 17
Ogden, Peter Skene, 145-47
Ojibway Indians, 15, 65
Oregon; see Columbia district
Oregon Treaty, 150
Orkneymen, 39-40, 61, 159
Ottawa River, 18

P

Pangman, Peter, 36
Patterson, Charles, 36, 45
Peace River, 45, 71, 86, 125
Pelly, A. E., 167
Pembina, 118, 168
pemmican, 53, 118-19, 159, 161
Piegan Indians, 88, 92-93
Pigeon River, 18, 52
Plains Indians, 53, 63, 65,
161-62; see also Assiniboine,
Blackfoot, Cree, Gros Ventres

Polk, James K., 149-50
Pond, Peter, 36, 42-47, 70-71
Pontiac, 35
postes du nord, 14-15
Prince Albert, Saskatchewan,
41, 55
Prince George, British
Columbia, 86
Prince Rupert, 24
Puget Sound, 142

R

Radisson, Pierre, 24-25, 26-27
Rainy Lake, 14, 18
Red River, 15, 53-54, 65, 162
Red River Colony, 129, 158-59;
brigades, 163-64; free traders,
167-69; origins, 116-17;
Pemmican War, 118-19;
Seven Oaks massacre, 120-22;
society, 157, 165-67, 171
Reindeer Lake, 84
Richardson, John, 80
Riel, Louis, 168
Robertson, Colin, 120, 123,
125-28, 129, 165
Rocky Mountain House, 88,
92-93
Ross, John, 45, 47
Rousseau, Dominic, 76-77
Rupert River, 25
Rupert's Land, 24, 172-74, 176
Russia, 147

S

St. Boniface, Manitoba, 158
St. Lawrence River, 10, 17, 23,
35, 43, 132